The social history of Canada

MIC

DATE DUE

A SOCIOLOGICAL STUDY OF A PORTION OF

THE CITY OF MONTREAL, CANADA

The city below the hill

HERBERT BROWN AMES

WITH AN INTRODUCTION BY P. F. W. RUTHERFORD

UNIVERSITY OF TORONTO PRESS

© University of Toronto Press 1972

Toronto and Buffalo

All rights reserved

ISBN (casebound) 0-8020-1878-5

ISBN (paperback) 0-8020-6142-7

Microfiche ISBN 0-8020-0216-1

LC 78-163831

Printed in the United States of America

This work first appeared as a book in 1897

An introduction

BY P. F. W. RUTHERFORD

UNDER THE SURFACE of the unparalleled prosperity of the age of Sir Wilfrid Laurier, Canada faced a gathering social crisis. Economic expansion had brought in its wake a wide assortment of new troubles – urban squalor, rural depopulation, the immigrant problem, 'big business,' public corruption, and the like. The press was filled with accounts of deepening uncertainty and confusion. From novels, magazines, conferences, and lectures poured a stream of comment on the new Canadian dilemma of material prosperity and social misery. On the eve of the Great War Clifford Sifton warned that the nation was following the same path as Europe and America, that one social problem was piled upon another, threatening the promise of 'the Canadian dream.'[1] Little wonder that some people, and not only rural apologists, yearned for the days of a simpler Canada.

A significant minority, drawn from the ranks of business and the professions, realized that the urban-industrial order was a permanent and even a welcome fact of Canadian life. Slowly they moved towards a new conception of the public interest, founded upon the pre-eminence of the community, a commitment to social order and social justice, and a firm belief in the twin ideals of economy and efficiency. Businessmen, journalists, and professionals combined their efforts to bring order to the chaos of city life. Such humanitarians as J. S. Woodsworth, backed by a host of church and women's organizations, mounted a campaign to rehabilitate, morally and socially, the immigrant and the underprivileged. Clifford Sifton headed a special advisory body, the Commission on Conservation, which was dedicated to the scientific exploitation of natural resources and the improvement of the urban and rural environments. Even Robert Borden, that 'colourless' Conservative leader, tried to bring this progressive spirit into national politics, though only with limited success.

Canadian 'progressivism' was heavily dependent upon similar movements in the United States and Great Britain. There was an intimate exchange of ideas and personnel throughout the North Atlantic community, so much so that it is often difficult to trace the national origin of any particular measure. Of course, the path of reform was different in all three countries. In contrast to the United States, Canadian reformers never founded a national organization like Teddy Roosevelt's Progressive party; rather, their efforts remained scattered among a myriad of organizations and institutions united only by a common concern for social problems. They were often opposed, and not only by vested interests. The reformers had to battle against public apathy and political indifference, constantly working for a new consensus which would support their advanced views. There were even a few critics who feared that the progressive spirit would destroy the individualistic ethos which supposedly underlay the Canadian community. Still, by 1920 the reformers and their ideas had drastically altered the character of the Canadian community.[2]

Sir Herbert Brown Ames (1863-1954) was one such reformer.[3] Born in Montreal of American parents and educated in three countries, he inherited a share in Ames-Holden Limited, a successful boot and shoe firm. After a short apprenticeship he became director of the family concern and later of a number of insurance companies including Great West Life. But he was not a typical member of the Montreal business establishment. His education gave him a wider knowledge of the outside world than many of his contemporaries. His entry into business circles had been easy, requiring little effort on his part. One suspects that Ames found his directorships a bit boring. Whatever the cause, Ames soon entered the arena of public affairs, which proved to be the abiding interest of his life. In 1892 he and a few other young men organized the Volunteer Electoral League to combat municipal corruption in Montreal.

Ames was much influenced by the example of American municipal reformers who were then engaged in a fierce struggle with 'bossism' in New York, Philadelphia, and Chicago. Although the situation in Montreal was not nearly so bad, the city was beginning to acquire a reputation for excessive civic corruption. The late nineteenth century had brought the rapid industrialization of Montreal (bringing its population to 267,000 by 1901). Economic growth attracted thousands of migrants from the countryside, many of whom swelled the ranks of the industrial proletariat. The city expanded away from the river edge and annexed nearby villages and suburbs. These changes reinforced the French character of Montreal, but they also fostered the segregation of the French and English, the rich and the poor, widening the social gulf between the various ethnic and economic groups within the community. In theory the city was controlled by an élite of anglophone businessmen and francophone professionals; in fact municipal politics was a fantastic mélange of opportunism, racism, partisanship, and class and neighbourhood loyalties. The political mechanism was lubricated by a free flow of money from office-seekers, franchise-holders, and construction men. In any case the expansion of civic services, especially utility franchises and local improvement schemes, provided aldermen with new opportunities for personal profit.

Ames initially hoped to choke off corruption by reforming the electoral character of municipal politics. He argued that there were only two kinds of municipal politicians, the 'good' and the 'bad.' He assumed that the electors would always pick the honest and able candidate when an election was run fairly. Under his leadership the Volunteer Electoral League, labelled 'the Kindergarten' by its critics, carried out a house-to-house canvass of five wards to compile an accurate voting list. The young men discovered some surprising anomalies: out of fifteen thousand electors, six hundred were incorrectly registered, four hundred were non-residents, three hundred were dead (some for decades), and forty-seven were minors. Most of these anomalies were cleared up — except where it was impossible to secure a death certificate. In February 1894, at the following civic election, the League endorsed various candidates, organized a force of volunteers, and patrolled the polling booths — all with considerable success. [4]

Ames admitted that he had built a reform machine to beat the 'old guard' at its own game. He himself served as an alderman from 1898 to 1906 and for four of those years as chairman of the municipal board of health. He wrote and lectured widely on the topic of municipal government, presided over the Good Government Association briefly, and carried out other 'good works' with the Protestant School Board, the Montreal YMCA, and various social agencies. Although Ames remained an advocate of 'collective action' as an instrument of social improvement and praised the efforts of civic organizations to mobilize the public will, his analysis of municipal problems gradually became more subtle. He now felt that good government rested as much upon a rational division of powers between legislative and administrative bodies as it did upon civic patriotism. In an address to the Canadian Club of Toronto (1903), he argued that the city council was essentially a legislative body, the mayor a 'people's tribune, the popular representative and critic.' [5]

Neither should interfere in administration. This task must be left to professional experts – a civic bureaucracy, trained to handle municipal affairs. Freed from political worries, such experts were able to give continuous attention to the details of city life. Of course, this structure would only work if the city council remained honest.

Montreal was not so fortunate. Ames' initial victories had opened a battle which lasted two decades between a broadly based reform coalition and an entrenched gang of politicians. In 1898 the reformers won a short-lived majority on council and a few years later even captured the mayoralty, but to little avail. In 1909 a provincial investigation by Justice Cannon discovered that for over a decade a large number of aldermen had been accepting bribes. His report concluded that the administration was 'saturated with corruption.' A shocked electorate very quickly endorsed a new governmental structure, which established the mayor and a four-man Board of Control as the municipal executive along the Toronto model. Further, they voted in 'le régime des hônnetes gens' to revamp the whole administration. During the next four years (1910-14), the new rulers did carry out some reforms, but proved unable to achieve either an economical or an efficient management of civic affairs. In 1914 the remaining reformers were crushed by the election as mayor of Médéric Martin, a colourful but unscrupulous cigarmaker who had been forced to resign his aldermanic seat after the Cannon investigation. Martin ushered in the modern era of municipal corruption in Montreal, unrelieved until the election of Jean Drapeau in 1954.[6]

Long before the débâcle of 1914, Ames had withdrawn from the municipal scene. In 1904 he was elected as a Conservative to the House of Commons for Montreal–St Antoine and retained his seat in each general election until his resignation in 1920. Within the party he acted as the spokesman and financial organizer for tory business interests in Montreal. He apparently favoured Borden's attempt to reform first the party and then the nation, although he was a vocal opponent of any scheme to turn over control of economic development to the state (he was especially critical of Borden's railway nationalization proposal of 1904). Ames' commitment to the progressive spirit was tempered by his belief in the efficacy of business enterprise. Prior to the 1911 election he was briefly the national organizer for the party, but he alienated new and old Conservatives, many of whom questioned his competence.[7] Because of his waning prestige he was not offered a portfolio by Borden after the Conservative victory. During the war he worked in a private capacity as the chairman of the National War Savings committee and as honorary secretary to the Canadian Patriotic Fund, two voluntary bodies concerned with the plight of the soldiers and their families.

Late in 1919 Ames accepted the position of financial director to the Secretariat of the League of Nations, one of the posts that had been 'assigned' to Canada as a member-state. This marked his permanent break with domestic politics, if not the Canadian scene. Ames welcomed the task of postwar reconstruction, and the search for a permanent international peace became the last real enthusiasm of his life. He believed the League was the only institution which could maintain the delicate European settlement; he hoped the success of the League would lead to a new 'concert of nations' founded upon debate and arbitration rather than military might.[8] After spending six years with the Secretariat he served as a Canadian delegate to the League Assembly in 1926. Because of his years of service to the League of Nations, he collected various honours from foreign governments – including the Order of Bountiful Crops (3rd class) from the Republic of China – but he received little recognition from his indifferent countrymen. In the following years he worked with private associations (at one time he was a lecturer for the Carnegie Endowment for International Peace) to formulate that elusive but essential 'public opinion' throughout the Anglo-American world which would foster the future international community. By the 1930s, however, his day had passed. A new generation of leaders, with different interests and assumptions, was in the ascendant. After almost four decades of activity, Ames retired and lived in obscurity until his death in 1954.

In 1904 a journalist described Ames as a representative of a new breed of men, more common in England than in North America – men who had deliberately forsaken commercial gain and a life of easy privilege to devote themselves to public affairs.[9] This observation was not wholly accurate. Ames did not reject his business background – and he certainly did not forsake 'commercial gain' or 'easy privilege.' He did, however, have a deep commitment to all levels of public life: civic, national, and international. He retained an implicit faith in the good will of the people and the ability of their leaders, but he was distressed by the waste and inefficiency of the old order. He championed the technique of rational organization, or, as he called it, 'collective action,' to mobilize and educate public opinion. He urged the creation of new bureaucratic structures to carry on the task of improvement long after the initial concern had disappeared. Neither of these approaches to reform clashed with the fundamental values of Canadian society. Ames was a manager, not a radical. Like most business reformers, he wanted to apply 'business principles' to social problems. Unfortunately he never realized his full potential. Although he participated in a variety of reform crusades, he lacked the stamina or the influence to carry his dreams to a satisfactory conclusion. Throughout his life he was forced to settle for second best, while others occupied the seats of power.

The City below the Hill was first published serially in the *Montreal Star* and later assembled as a book.[10] Because of its local significance the book received slight attention outside Montreal; after the initial flurry of comment it was remembered only as an early piece of writing by a prominent public man. This was unfortunate.

The book was a detailed investigation of social conditions in a portion of west-end Montreal, bounded by Westmount, the city limits, and the St Lawrence river. The resident population (some 38,000) included sizeable elements of all three nationalities: French Canadian, Irish Canadian, and English (or 'British') Canadian. None the less Ames argued that the section had a definite social and economic character. Although the city below the hill did contain a poor element – centred in 'Griffintown' and 'the Swamp' – and a few professional and salaried men, its character was determined by the craftsman, the factory worker, and the clerk, or what Ames called 'the real industrial class.' He had, in fact, picked an area representative of working-class life in Montreal.

Hitherto the industrial class had received little attention. Ames argued that the wealthy and the workers existed in two different worlds: the wealthy knew more about the slums of London, the beggars of Paris, and the tenement houses of New York than about the unfortunate social conditions in their midst. Such ignorance was inexcusable. The city was an organic whole, a single community, its well-being dependent upon the health and happiness of all citizens; the terrifying smallpox epidemic of 1885 had so obviously demonstrated this. As the natural civic leaders, the wealthy had a responsibility to improve the community. Ames hoped his book would remedy their ignorance and illustrate the feasibility of reform.

Though unique in Canada, Ames' study was only a minor entry in a long list of similar works already published in the United States and Great Britain. It seems that *The City below the Hill* was modelled upon some of the more ambitious of these works, notably Charles Booth's mammoth analysis of life in London.[11] Thus it is hardly surprising that Ames did not diverge very far from the new reform orthodoxy popular outside Canada. He was not striving for originality but for accuracy. He constantly compared conditions in Montreal with those in European and American cities. The urban crisis was an international problem. He believed, however, that because of the relative youth of Canadian cities the evils of poor housing had not taken such deep root as in Europe and America, and therefore could be more easily reversed. Perhaps it was a naïve assumption, but it became common in urban reform circles throughout Canada during the next decade.

Ames stuffed his book with facts. By the late nineteenth century statistical analysis enjoyed a considerable vogue among the new social scientists because it seemed able to rationalize the increasingly complex world created by the urban-industrial order. Ames did not question this assumption. To ensure 'scientific' information, he organized a house-to-house canvass of the city below the hill, a technique borrowed from the experience of the Volunteer Electoral League. The enumerators were armed with a lengthy questionnaire relating to employment, family make-up, housing, rent, ethnic background, and so on. Their results were tabulated under ten specific headings and transferred to a series of maps. Ames assumed the whole process would provide a composite picture of the environment of the industrial class. But his pursuit of statistical truth became an end in itself. Some of his terms, such as those peculiar 'labour units,' were needlessly complicated. Too often he lost sight of his goal in a welter of figures and calculations. His study was at its best when he allowed his own fears and beliefs to intrude, as in his description of housing conditions.

Ames was aware that the city below the hill housed a 'submerged tenth,' the poor who did not enjoy a 'decent subsistence.' He defined the poor as those families who earned less than $260 a year, and therefore were unable to purchase the necessities of housing, food, and clothing. Breaking with conventional wisdom he claimed that the proportion of the 'undeserving poor,' the drunk and the lazy, was not nearly as large as many imagined. True, drunkenness was rife in 'Griffintown' and 'the Swamp' (roughly one liquor outlet for every 160 persons), but intemperance was as much a symptom as a cause of poverty. Ames believed that poverty was a social condition, fostered by insufficient and irregular employment. If given the opportunity, the poor would work to escape slum life. This was a novel conclusion in 1897.

But Ames was not a social reformer in the tradition of J.S. Woodsworth. He was much more concerned with the plight of the workers than with the condition of the poor. To his mind the quality of city life now depended less upon the wealth and culture of its leading citizens and more upon the moral and physical character of the working class. Since Ames-Holden Limited was located in the heart of the city below the hill, he had a certain proprietory interest in the well-being of labour. His company was among the first to recognize a shop union as a bargaining agent and to use the union label on its products.[12] Ames warned that industrial expansion had worked a social revolution by undermining the economic significance of the countryside. It was inevitable that the city would continue to grow in size and influence. Although hardly a romantic, Ames foresaw that the industrial proletariat would become the backbone of the new Canada.

Even though Ames believed this proletariat was a single social and economic class, he did deal with the obvious problem of Montreal's ethnicity. 'Race characteristics' had some impact upon social habits. Ames admitted that the British Canadians enjoyed a better standard of living, if only by default. 'For density and high death rate the French-Canadians take undesirable precedence; for overcrowding and poverty the Irish-Canadian sections make the least creditable showing' (p. 95). But further speculation was dangerous. Ames steadfastly refused to pander to the already widespread belief among the wealthy in British-Canadian superiority. He was convinced that the problems faced by the inhabitants of the city below the hill were defined by environment, not ethnicity. However refreshing his attitude, he did not investigate the pattern of neighbourhood life (the habits, ambitions, and fears of each ethnic group), and this failure leaves his conclusion open to serious doubt.

Virtually all reformers were agreed that the countryside was much healthier than the city. Density, congestion, overcrowding, the common 'evils' of life in the industrial city, were injurious to the urban dweller, especially to women and children. Though some writers doubted that this situation could be remedied, Ames was not among them. He reasoned that with the advance of industrial technology the city need not be an unhealthy place for anyone to live. In 1897 this was hardly true of Montreal. The health of a city was judged by the size of its death-rate: not only was Montreal's rate higher than that of London, Rome, and Brussels, but it fluctuated according to the social and economic character of each ward. In their districts the wealthy enjoyed good housing, spacious streets, parks, and modern sanitary conveniences. The proletariat did not. Here was the most telling proof of discrimination against the underprivileged.

Ten years before it would win general support among Canadian reformers, Ames was influenced by the concept of town planning and urban renewal. He was incensed by the prevalence of the outdoor privy, 'that sanitary abomination,' in working-class neighbourhoods – he even kept a map in his office recording the distribution of outhouses across the city. As long as they endured, they threatened the public health and character of Montreal. Similarly, Ames condemned the 'rear tenements' (fronting behind or to one side of the street), because, while they satisfied a need for cheap housing among the poor, they were rarely fit for rental. 'If one desires to find where drunkenness and crime, disease and death, poverty and distress are most in evidence in western Montreal, he has only to search out the rear tenements (p. 45). Ames was troubled by the experience of New York, where reformers were already engaged in a fierce (and not altogether promising) battle with tenement landlords. Fortunately many Montreal workers were housed in small buildings with adequate ventilation and a reasonable amount of room space. Such residences fostered the 'home influence' which preserved the moral values and the self-reliance of the wage-earners.

The ideal home, however, was one 'where the front door is used by but one family, where the house faces upon a through street, where water-closet accommodation is provided, and where there are as many rooms allotted to a family as there are persons composing it (p. 40). It was a very specific goal. In effect, Ames favoured a minimum housing standard throughout Montreal, which would ensure a decent environment for the industrial class and the poor.

After such a detailed analysis, Ames' actual proposals for civic improvement seem peculiarly limited. By instinct, he was opposed to radical change. He expected the city council to enforce existing housing laws and to extend sanitary facilities. But because the state had 'no right to take chances with the peoples' money,' he hoped to persuade businessmen to finance a variety of cheap, sturdy houses for rent to the poor and the industrial worker. He appealed to their better nature and the profit motive – thus his reference to the motto 'philanthropy and five per cent,' which had long been popular in the United States.[13] These housing projects would change the whole character of the city below the hill. They would create a happy and energetic work force situated within easy reach of the growing industries of west-end Montreal. Ames himself built a group of model apartments for some thirty-nine families, which combined low rents with pleasant, comfortable surroundings. Unfortunately the Diamond Court project was too small to have much impact upon the general housing situation and Ames' business compatriots did not respond to his pleas. He could hardly have expected this failure since private philanthropy still seemed in 1897 to be viable as an instrument of social improvement. Even in the next decade reformers remained convinced that town planning was heavily dependent upon business initiative. Not until the postwar reconstruction era did people admit the state had some responsibility for new housing, and only then because of the plight of the returned soldiers.

The City below the Hill is a pioneer work in the field of urban sociology in Canada. Ames was little affected by the rural nostalgia which was a common theme in much comment on the urban crisis. Earlier than most of his contemporaries, he recognized that the city was the natural habitat of a growing portion of the Canadian population. He moved tentatively towards the concept of an urban ecology, the belief that the city was an organism defined by a myriad of social and economic phenomena; but his forte was empirical research, not philosophy. He was concerned primarily with the economic and material characteristics of urban life, particularly as they related to class. True, he never overcame the paternalist assumptions of the business community around him; but he hardly fits the stereotype of the Montreal capitalist. His labours were inspired by a genuine sympathy for the underprivileged and a vision of a new industrial order. Within his work were the germs of the town planning and social welfare movements that were later to change the urban landscape. However incomplete, his book depicts the life of a working-class community after the first years of rapid industrialization. And it warns against the practice of making too many generalizations, whether about working-class misery or business callousness.

NOTES

1 'Address of Welcome,' *Proceedings of the Sixth National Conference on City Planning* (Boston, 1914), pp. 5-13.
2 Only recently have historians begun to consider the social crisis and the progressive spirit in the Laurier era: J. Levitt, *Henri Bourassa and the Golden Calf* (Ottawa, 1969); R. Allen, 'The Social Gospel and the Reform Tradition in Canada, 1880-1928,' *Canadian Historical Review,* LIX (Dec. 1968), pp. 381-99; Carl Berger, *The Sense of Power: Studies in the Ideas of Canadian Imperialism, 1867-1914* (Toronto, 1970), pp. 177-98; R. Cook, 'Stephen Leacock and the Age of Plutocracy,' in J. Moir, ed., *Character and Circumstance* (Toronto, 1970), pp. 163-81; R. C. Brown, 'The Political Ideas of Robert Borden,' in M. Hamelin, ed., *The Political Ideas of the Prime Ministers of Canada* (Ottawa, 1969), pp. 87-97.
3 The bare facts of Ames' life are drawn from H. J. Morgan, *Canadian Men and Women of the Time,* 1912, p. 22; *Canadian Who's Who,* 1954, pp. 15-16; and W. A. Atherton, *Montreal from 1535 to 1914,* III (Montreal, 1914), pp. 618-20.
4 H. B. Ames, 'The "Machine" in Honest Hands,' *Canadian Magazine,* III, 1894, pp. 101-9.

5 H. B. Ames, 'Some Problems of Municipal Government,' *Proceedings of the Canadian Club, Toronto,* I, 1903-4, pp. 89-91.
6 For a more extensive treatment of the downfall of reform in Montreal, see J. I. Cooper, *Montreal: A Brief History* (Montreal, 1969), pp. 131-44.
7 I am indebted to Mr John English for allowing me to consult a series of letters from the Borden collection he has uncovered which outline Ames' career within the Conservative party.
8 For an elaboration of these ideas, see two pamphlets by Ames: 'Address,' League of Nations Society in Canada, 1922, and 'Seven Years with the League of Nations,' Henry Ward Beecher Foundation Lectures, Amherst College, 1927.
9 A. R. Carman, 'Canadian Celebrities: No. 53 – Herbert Brown Ames,' *Canadian Magazine,* XXIII, 1904, p. 308.
10 Montreal: The Bishop Engraving and Printing Company, 1897.
11 Charles Booth, also a business reformer, had begun a research project in the 1880s which eventually resulted in seventeen volumes on the 'Life and Labour of the People in London.' See Harold W. Pfautz, 'Introduction,' *Charles Booth on the City* (Chicago, 1967), pp. 3-170.
12 Cooper, *Montreal,* p. 89.
13 For a discussion of the American movement, see Stanley Buder, *Pullman* (New York, 1967), pp. 28-45.

The city below the hill

HERBERT BROWN AMES

Contents

Chapter 1

Introduction

The situation and boundaries of 'the city below the hill' / Comparison
with 'the city above the hill' / How the figures for these articles were
obtained / Why this district was selected / Lines upon which this
sociological investigation has been pursued / Purpose of these articles

IF ONE were to draw a line across the map of a portion of the city of Montreal, following Lagauchetiere street from its junction with Bleury street to the Windsor Station and thence along the tracks of the C.P.R. as far as the city limits, he would divide the south-western half of our city into two occupied districts of nearly equal extent. One of these districts, that to the west, is upon high ground; the other, that to the east, is in the main but little above the river level. The former region, for lack of a better name, we shall call 'The city above the hill,' the latter, in contrast therefrom, 'The city below the hill.' To pass from the former into the latter it is necessary to descend a considerable hill and with this descent becomes noticeable a marked change in the character of the inhabitants and in the nature of their surroundings. Looking down from the mountain top upon these two areas, the former is seen to contain many spires, but no tall chimneys, the latter is thickly sprinkled with such evidences of industry and the air hangs heavy with their smoke.

'The city above the hill' is the home of the classes. Within its well-built residences will be found the captains of industry, the owners of real estate, and those who labor with brain rather than hand. Here in predominating proportion reside the employing, the professional and the salaried classes. The manual worker in this district is indeed rare, the home of the poor cannot there be found. It is the exclusive habitat of the rich and of the well-to-do.

'The city below the hill,' on the other hand, is the dwelling place of the masses. Here it is the rich man that one finds it difficult to discover. Salaried and professional men are not entirely lacking, but even when to their number are added the shop-keepers and hotel men, these together represent but 15 per cent of its population. 'The city below the hill' is the home of the craftsman, of the manual wage-earner, of the mechanic and the clerk, and three-quarters of its population belong to this, the real industrial class. *This* area is not without its poor, and, as in other cities, a submerged tenth is present with its claims upon neighborly sympathy.

Most of the residents of the upper city know little – and at times seem to care less – regarding their fellow-men in the city below. To many of the former the condition of the latter is as little known as that of natives in Central Africa. With many of the upper city all that they regard as of interest to or with effect upon their daily life is located either in the section wherein they reside or that wherein their daily business is transacted. To pass from the one to the other only well-ordered thoroughfares are travelled. From this beaten track they seldom wander and of other regions they possess little or no knowledge. At this time in the world's history, when careful observers and honest thinkers in every land are coming more and more to realize what is meant by the interdependence of society, when those who study city life are each day more fully persuaded that ordinary urban conditions are demoralizing and that no portion of the community can be allowed to deteriorate without danger to the whole, when it is being proven over and over again by enlightened municipalities that the public health can be conserved, morals improved and lives saved by a right knowledge of local conditions and the proper use of measures for their amelioration, it is opportune that the citizens of Montreal should, for a time, cease discussing the slums of London, the beggars of Paris and the tenement house evils of New York and endeavor to learn something about themselves and to understand more perfectly the conditions present in their very midst.

During the autumn and early winter of 1896, in an endeavor to obtain accurate information along certain sociological lines for at least a limited portion of the city of Montreal, a house-to-house canvass was made of the district already entitled 'the city under the hill.' An unofficial industrial census was taken by experienced men of the area lying within the following boundaries: On the west Lagauchetiere street and the Canadian Pacific tracks, on the north St. Alexander and McGill streets, on the east Centre street and a line extended in the same direction as far as the river, and on the south the city limits and Laprairie street. If one were to take a city map and describe thereon an oblong by means of lines connecting the following points, viz., intersection of the C.P.R. by the city limits, St. Patrick's church, the middle of the guard pier, and St. Gabriel church, he would fairly enclose the area selected for examination. This district, including part of the canals and wharves, parks, streets, etc., is about a square mile in extent and includes 475 acres dedicated to purposes of business or residence. Since nearly thirty-eight thousand persons dwell and about seventeen thousand persons labor therein, we have here sufficient material to enable us to strike reasonable averages and form fair conclusions. The enumerators were instructed to obtain information upon the following points: regarding each place of employment, the number of workers and their division into men, women, and children; regarding each residence the number of families therein, number of rooms per family, number of persons in family and the proportion thereof of adults, school children, young children and lodgers, the rental paid, the wages earned, the sanitary accommodation, the nationality, the religious belief and other similar matters. The figures thus gathered were then carefully combined and tabulated. For purposes of comparison 'the city below the hill' was also divided into thirty sections and the averages for each section worked out. This material forms the basis of the series of articles which, accompanied by illustrative maps, appear in this pamphlet.

There are reasons why the region selected is especially adapted to sociological investigation. It is naturally homogeneous, not as to nationalities, but as to the social scale of its residents. It is a district the boundaries of which conform with natural conditions. Climb the hill, crossing anywhere our western limit, and one emerges at once into the habitat of the upper middle class. Cross McGill street and one is forthwith among warehouses and office buildings, wherein no residential population can be found. Beyond Centre street lies that special district of Point St. Charles, which is almost an independent suburb by itself, being sustained by employment furnished in the offices and workshops of the G.T.R. Only to the southward, as one crosses Laprairie street, or that imaginary line – in the vicinity of Fulford and Dominion streets – which separates the city from Ste Cunegonde, does one ask why our census stopped here rather than at a point beyond.

One more consideration gives to the study of this section an added interest. The wage-earners among our people are drawn almost exclusively from three nationalities, the French-Canadian, the Irish-Canadian, and the British-Canadian. In this district, and in no other considerable area throughout the entire city, are these three nationalities blended together in not very unequal proportions. The study of any other working-class region would be the study of but one predominating nationality. Here we can study a class rather than a race.

Satisfied then that the district selected is one especially adapted to give returns which may fairly be taken to represent industrial Montreal and may be used when comparing figures with other cities, let me in closing this introductory outline give the topics under which will be treated the material made available by this census.

2 Employment, where furnished and to what extent
3 The composition of the typical family
4 Family incomes and workers' wages
5 The homes of the industrial class
6 Comparative rentals
7 Density of population and overcrowding in the home
8 The poor of the 'West End'
9 The death rate and some of its lessons
10 Nationalities, their location and distribution

There are among the dwellers of 'the city above the hill' not a few, we believe, who have the welfare of their fellow-men at heart, who realize that there is no influence more elevating than the proper home, who acknowledge that there is need for improvement in the matter of housing the working classes of this city, and who would be willing to assit any movement of a semi-philanthropic character having for its object the erection of proper homes for the families of working men. These persons are business men. They are not those who take things for granted. They require to have demonstrated to them in black and white the local need for action and the conditions – changing with every locality – to which it would be needful to conform to meet the needs of the case, and, at the same time, yield reasonable financial returns.

For such as these this series of articles is especially intended. I hope before many months to be able to supplement it with still another paper, demonstrating, from actual experiment, that 'Philanthropy and 5 per cent' in Montreal, as elsewhere, can be combined.

Map A

"THE CITY B

ABOVE = POPULATION

BELOW = N° OF PER

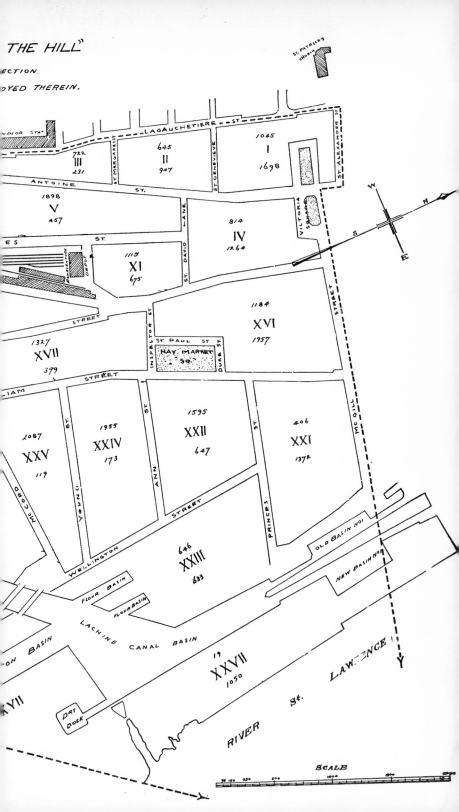

Chapter 2

Employment

Why this should be the first matter considered / The figures on map B explained / The four questions considered / 1 As to what portions of the lower city are employing and what residential / 2 Where the chief industrial establishments are located and the amount of employment they furnish / 3 As to the character of the work, the proportion of women and children and the kinds of labor upon which they are employed / 4 As to whether the district furnishes homes for all therein employed / Conclusion: why this section is eminently fitted for philanthropic investment

ONE OF the first matters worthy of consideration in our study of 'the city below the hill' is the location and distribution, the quantity and character of the employment therein furnished. We have already learned that the district furnishes homes for nearly thirty-eight thousand persons, and we now further desire to ascertain where and how these residents secure that employment whereby they are enabled to subsist. In choosing a home, all other circumstances being equal, the wage-earner prefers to locate in the vicinity of his daily work, and, therefore, unless counteracting conditions are found to exist, the prevalence of centres of large employment will be accompanied by an abundance of dwellings not far distant.

Map B shows the area under consideration divided into thirty sections for purposes of comparative examination. Certain figures will be noticed inscribed within the limits of each section and these first demand explanation. Just above the Roman letters which designate the section is set forth the number of places therein furnishing employment. Every establishment, from the large factory with several hundred workmen to the corner grocery which employs but one clerk, is here included as a place of employment. To the left of the section number is found the totality of persons therein employed, to the right the number of 'labor units'* thereby represented. In the centre we have the number of 'labor units' per acre, and below this again the average number of 'labor units' for each place of employment. Finally in the lower right hand corner of the section is a plus or minus quantity representing the excess or lack of wage-workers employed compared with wage-earners resident within the given section. The meaning of the figures on the map can be made clearer by illustration: Take section 1 as an example. We

---

* The term 'labor unit' is to be thus understood: A man is taken as the unit of measurement. A woman is regarded as representing ½ and a child ¼ of this unit. Thus four persons, one man, one woman and two children would represent two 'labor units.' Where the number of 'labor units,' as in section 10, is nearly equal to the number employed, it is obvious that woman and child labor in this section exist to a very inconsiderable extent; when, however, as is the case in section 2, there is apparent a great difference between the left and right hand numbers, this signifies that here many women and children find work.

find that there are within its boundaries 60 places of employment, wherein 1698 persons, represented by 1465 'labor units' are employed; that this section gives employment at the rate of $125\frac{2}{10}$ 'labor units' per acre of territory; that on an average $24\frac{4}{10}$ 'labor units' are assignable to each establishment; and lastly that 1441 *more* wage-earners obtain work within its limits than reside therein.

From these data we are enabled, by comparing the corresponding figures of the several sections, to draw definite conclusions upon the following matters:

1 As to what sections throughout the district may be termed 'employing' and what 'residential' and the location of these in groups.

2 As to the location and distribution of the larger industrial establishments and the amount of employment furnished throughout the 'employing belt.'

3 As to the character of the employment and the proportionate amount therein of woman and child labor.

4 As to whether the city under the hill employs more persons than it supplies with homes.

1 The total number of places of labor throughout the entire area of 'the city below the hill' is reckoned at 1442. In these establishments 16,237 persons find work, a figure represented by 14,289 'labor units.' This does not include the employers, who would probably number 2000 more. Coming to the first aspect of the question, viz., the separation of the sections into those of employment and those of residence, we observe at once that no section within the district fails to furnish at least some employment, though the amount may vary greatly from 1588 units in section 16 to 3 units in section 9. If we arrange the sections in their order between these extremes as follows: $16 - 1 - 21 - 4 - 29 - 27 - 11 - 23 - 2 - 22 - 20 - 19 - 5 - 30 - 17 - 28 - 26 - 3 - 13 - 24 - 18 - 14 - 8 - 12 - 25 - 7 - 10 - 6 - 15 - 9$, we find that the first sixteen sections above quoted (alone excluding section 17) provide employment for 14,000 persons, that is to say, contain 90 per cent of all the employment furnished. In each of the fourteen remaining sections the number of persons employed is less than the number of wage-earners resident therein. The former group

Map B.

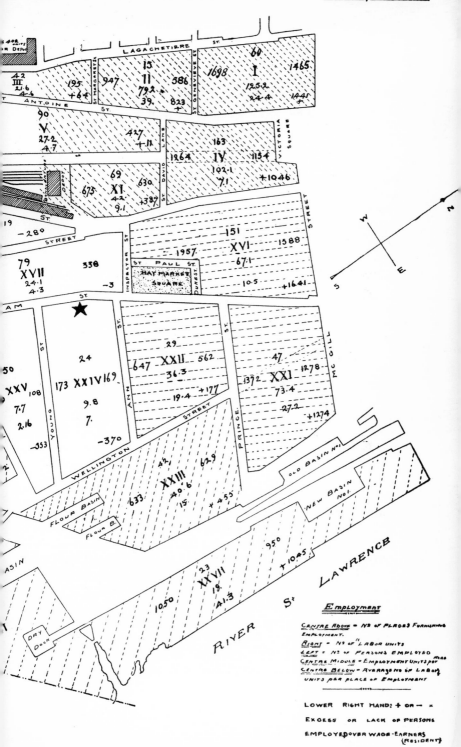

of sections therefore, which have been distinguished upon the map by means of parallel broken lines, may rightly be characterized as 'employing' and the latter as 'residential' localities.

The location of these 'employing' sections is readily apparent. They will be found to occupy the northern and eastern portions of our lower city. A band of territory not unlike a broad fish-hook, with its point at Windsor street, its back at McGill street, and its shank following the banks of the canal, will include the 'employing' sections of the district. There are a few places of employment lying outside of this belt, but only four of these provide work for over 100 employes, not more than twenty employ over 25 persons, and, with exception of sections 24 and 6, nowhere outside of the 'employing belt' will the establishments of any section average 5 'labor units' each.

2 And now, secondly, as to the location and distribution of the industrial establishments throughout the 'employing belt' and the amount of employment by them furnished.

The district which lies between Lagauchetiere and Notre Dame streets, stretching from St. Alexander to Windsor streets, comprising sections 1, 2, 4, 11 and parts of 3 and 5 (but not including Windsor Station) in proportion to its extent furnishes more employment than any other throughout the lower city. Here are employed 4927 persons, equivalent to 4160 'labor units,' which gives an average of 80 'labor units' per acre. In this group of sections are situated no less than 40 places of considerable employment, establishments credited with at least 25 'labor units.' Chief among these are E. A. Small & Co.'s wholesale clothing establishment, and the shoe factories of The Ames-Holden Co. (Ltd.), Jas. Linton & Co., and Geo. T. Slater & Sons in section 1; also the shirt factories of Tooke Bros. and A. H. Sims & Co., with the Lang Manf'g Co., makers of confectionery, etc., in section 2. Besides these, several prominent firms of roofers, plumbers, makers of electrical supplies, etc., employing considerable labor, are to be found in this locality.

That district which is made up of sections 16, 21 and 22 ranks next in importance, judged by the number of 'labor units' per acre. This group may be credited with 3428 units, or 61 to the acre. Herein the nature of the employment varies greatly. In section 16 the wholesale clothing establishment of H. Shorey & Co., the shoe factory of The Whitham Manf'g Co., and J. M. Fortier's cigar factory are the most important. In section 21, along McGill street, are to be found the cigar factories of Jacobs & Co., and Tasse, Wood & Co., Tester & Co.'s candy manufactory, the establishment of the Montreal Biscuit Co., and G. H. Harrower's shirt factory, all employment centres of considerable importance. Southward from McGill street are Watson, Foster & Co.'s wall paper factory, Miller Bros. & Toms' machine shop, Ives & Co.'s foundry, and the several works of the Royal Electric Co., with a number of lesser foundries and machine shops. Esplin's box factory on Duke street, and Davis' tobacco factory on Dalhousie street, are the last outposts of considerable employment as one penetrates the residential portion of 'Griffintown.'

Sections 23 and 27, which enclose the canal basin, furnish employment to the amount of 1579 'labor units,' but owing to the extent of these sections the average will not exceed 25 units per acre. Section 23 contains the machine shops and metal working establishments of J. & R. Weir, Robert Gardner & Sons, W. C. White, and others. Beyond the canal in section 27 are the extensive nail works of Peck, Benny & Co., Pillow, Hersey & Co., and the Canada Horse Nail Company. Ogilvy's Royal flour mills, the Malleable Iron Company's works, and the headquarters of the Sicily Asphalt Co. are also to be found here. In summer time one hundred men are employed about the locks and the canal basin, engaged in unloading the regular river boats; the Government dry dock and the various coal companies along the canal also are considerable employers of labor. (The G.T.R. offices and shops, although these employ about 2000 men exclusive of trainmen, etc., are omitted from this calculation.)

Continuing along the east bank of the canal one finds half a dozen extensive establishments between Wellington and Laprairie streets. In this district the Canada Sugar Refinery is the largest employer of labor. Next in order come Pillow, Hersey & Co.'s rolling mills, Belding, Paul & Co.'s silk mills, the rope-walk of the Consumers' Cordage Co., the works of the Canada Switch and Spring Co., J. W. Windsor's cannery, and the James Shearer Co.'s sash and door factory. These, together with several lesser establishments in this district, will aggregate 1779 'labor units,' or 23 to each acre of territory.

The last district for examination in this manner is that comprising
sections 26, 19 and 20, lying west of the canal, from Wellington
bridge to the city limits. The northern portion of this district
contains several box factories and planing mills, and the new station
of the Standard Light and Power Co. In the vicinity of the Seigneurs
street bridge are MacDougall's foundry and Ogilvy's Glenora flour
mills. Southwest of these are the Montreal woollen mills, the works
of the Canada Paint Co., Grier's lumber yards, and on the Ste
Cunegonde boundary line, the factory of the Singer Sewing Machine
Co. This district claims in all 1392 'labor units' or 25 to the acre.

3 We will next investigate the matter of the proportionate
amount of woman and child labor throughout 'the city below the
hill,' and ask where and for what purposes this labor is employed. Of
the total number of persons to be found in its industrial establishments of all kinds, 12,511 or 77 per cent are men, 3266 or 20 per
cent are women and 460 or 3 per cent are boys and girls. In order to
discover those sections wherein women and child labor is in larger
proportion we have only to note where there is considerable
disparity between the total number employed and the number of
'labor units' as set forth upon the map. In sections 1, 2, 3, 16, 17,
18, 20, 22, 27, 28 and 30 this difference is most noticeable. In
section 1, where are the clothing and shoe factories, about 25 per
cent of those employed are women and children. In section 2, which
contains the shirt factories, 75 per cent of the workers are of this
character. Section 16, because of the clothing, shoe and cigar
factories within its boundaries, will be found employing, out of
1957 persons, 730 or 37 per cent that are women and child workers.
That section 21 and 22 contain 13 per cent and 28 per cent
respectively of labor other than adult male, is due again to the
presence of cigar and shirt factories. In the sections between William
street and the canal female labor is rare owing to the heavy nature of
the employment. Beyond the canal, out of 3052 persons employed
in sections 27 to 30, 253 are women and 270 are boys and girls. This
is about 17 per cent of the whole number there at work. Both
women and children may be found in considerable numbers in the
nail works. The silk manufactory, the cannery and the bag works
employ many women; the sugar refinery employs boys and the rope
walk and the paint works many boys and girls. The only establishment immediately west of the canal largely employing this kind of

labor is in section 20, viz.: the Montreal Woollen Mills, where 100 women are to be found. Several other sections, such as 17 and 18, contain a high comparative percentage of this labor, but the number of persons in reality is not great. When the industrial census, upon which these articles are based, was taken, grown lads capable of doing a man's work, were counted as men even though not yet of age. This needs to be borne in mind as these have been excluded from among the child workers. Our 'city below the hill,' then, taken as a representative locality, goes to prove that in Montreal the proportion of woman and child workers is not nearly so high as in the old land. But a little over one out of every five of our industrial workers belong to this category and of this fact we may be justly proud.

4 Our fourth theme is worthy of consideration before we close this study upon employment in the district of our selection. When our special census returns were totalled, it was found that while 16,237 persons secured regular work in the industrial establishments of the district, only 10,853 wage-earners were reported as belonging to the 7671 families therein resident. The inference from this fact is that at least 5384 wage-earners of the district with their families have homes outside of it. To ascertain the correctness of this hypothesis, the main avenues leading north, east and south were watched for several evenings at about six o'clock and those passing each way were counted. The contents of the West Ward debouches into McGill street, passes up Beaver Hall or Windsor street, and but little of it remains for the night within 'the city below the hill.' Four people come up McGill street and turn north for every one that comes down on his way toward 'Griffintown.' Three persons turn north along Craig street for every one who goes south. Standing at the intersections of St. Antoine, St. James or Notre Dame streets by the city limits, one remarks that a constant stream pours outward towards Ste Cunegonde and St. Henri, while few are those who are inward bound. The travel across Wellington bridge is nearly the same both ways, though there is a slight excess of inward bound. The employes of the G.T.R. shops going northwest from Centre street are counterbalanced by those going southeast. There can, therefore, be little doubt but that, for reasons which we may later on consider, *fully one third of those employed during the day within our district pass out of it when the day's work is done.* Is it wise to endeavor to

keep these persons within the district, near to their work, or shall we encourage them to become citizens of outlying municipalities?

We shall in future articles learn something regarding the residential conditions which obtain throughout 'the city below the hill.' It is sufficient, however, for our present purpose to have shown that the district is capable of sustaining, by means of the industries therein operated, a much larger number of families than it at present contains, and to affirm that, with suitable dwellings and proper civic regulations, every wage-worker employed therein might also live in comfort and health within easy walking distance of his daily work. This conclusion would seem to indicate that, if some central spot were chosen (as that starred upon the map, which is within half a mile or ten minutes' walk of industrial establishments employing over 12,000 persons), buildings thereon erected, if suitable and of reasonable rental, would not long want for occupants, could not fail to be a benefit to the workingmen and should form an investment for the capitalist at once safe and profitable. This starred spot has been chosen and here the experiment will have a fair trial. Of the result I will have more to say later.

Chapter 3

The composition of the family

HAVING investigated, in the previous article, the subject of the
employment furnished throughout the district under examination,
we next turn from the study of the workshop to the study of the
home, and offer a few considerations upon matters affecting family
life.

Two phases of this subject naturally present themselves, since two
things are necessary to every home, the examination of the family
occupying and of the habitation occupied. This article is on the
former theme and is to treat of the composition of the family as it
will be found to exist in 'the city below the hill.' More fully
explained our task is to ascertain (1) the size of the average family
and the local variations from this standard, (2) the component parts
of the average family and the greater or lesser proportion of the
several elements in certain localities. We will also incidentally
endeavor to discover and trace the operation of several natural laws;
the object of the whole study being to guide us to a right
appreciation of proper residential requirements for families according to the several localities.

In the first place we will make a statistical presentation of the
available data from which we are to draw our conclusions. In the
city below the hill dwell 7671 families. These families include
37,652 persons. Of these persons, 25,051 are from sixteen years of
age upwards and may be by us regarded as adults. These 25,051
adults are divisible into three classes: the wage-earners, male and
female numbering 10,853; the home-tenders reckoned at 11,720;
and the lodgers, who either may or may not be wage earners, in
number 2478. If we subtract the adults from the total number of
persons, the remainder, amounting in number to 12,601, will
represent the children, and this number is again divisible into
children of school age of whom there are 6948 and young children
of whom there are 5653.

What then is the composition of the typical family? Though it
may appear strange to the eye, this can best be accurately expressed
in terms of decimals. The average family contains 4.90 persons. Of
this number 1.41 work for wages and are the family's support; 1.53
remain at home and contribute more or less to its care. To every
third family there is assignable one lodger, who helps to swell the
family income, but who, further than this, does not enter into our
calculations. The average home contains 1.64 children; .91 is of
school age, while .73 is an infant in the house.

These proportions may perhaps be expressed more vividly if we imagine a block to contain thirty such families. We should then expect to find in this block 147 persons, 42 of whom would be wage-earners; 46 of whom would be home-tenders; 10 of whom would be lodgers; 49 of whom would be children, of these latter 27 being of school age and 22 being infants at home. We might carry the analysis of the wage-earning portion still further. We noted in our study on employment that 77 per cent of those employed were men and grown boys; 20 per cent children. Of the 42 wage-earners above cited we might reasonably expect that 33 would be grown males, 8 would be women and one a child.

That there will be considerable variation from the average family, when we come to a comparative examination of the figures peculiar to the several sections, is clearly evident. These differences are shown by map C to be studied in connection with this article. By way then of explaining the accompanying map let it be stated that the figures directly over the Roman letters denote — carried to the second decimal — the average family for that section; that the figures to the left represent the adult portion of this average family, the number above signifying the proportion of wage-earners, the figures below the number of home-tenders; that the figures to the right show, when totalled, the entire number of children in the average family, the number above representing the proportion of school children and that below the proportion of young children; that the figures immediately under the Roman letters indicate the proportion of lodgers which would fall to each family of the section were it possible for these to be evenly distributed; and finally, that the figures at the very bottom, within each section, express the typical family of that locality after the 'lodger element' has been eliminated.

We have seen that the average family, all included, contains 4.90 persons. Upon examining the map we are struck by the fact that in several sections it very considerably exceeds this figure. The conspicuous sections in this regard are 2, 1, 5, 3 and 11. These sections contain numerous boarding houses, and 20 per cent of their population are lodgers. Now it is obvious that the presence in certain sections of such a considerable proportion of an element not truly an integral part of the real family, and the absence of this element in other sections, renders comparisons unfair until the lodgers have, from all calculations, been eliminated. This accomplished, these several sections, previously accredited with unusually large families,

Map C.

Above = No. of Persons in Average Family

Middle = No. of Lodgers

Below = The Average Family Less Lodgers

COMPOSITION OF THE FAMILY

LEFT = { Above = No of WAGE-EARNERS, IN AVERAGE FAMILY
         Below = No of HOME-TENDERS.

RIGHT = { Above = No of SCHOOL CHILDREN, IN AVERAGE FAMILY
          Below = No of YOUNG CHILDREN,

will not now be found greatly to differ from the others, while *our typical family group will contain 4.6 (4.59) souls.*

Now, while the fact and extent of the variation between the several sections is readily apparent, by the aid of the map, in respect to such matters as the size of the family, the prevalence of lodgers, the increase or decrease in the wage-earning as well as the home-tending element, the number of the children and the relative proportion of school to infant population, it is a task far more difficult to point out any reasonable explanation for these divergencies. This is probably due to the fact that our 'city below the hill' contains a population which, in the matter of social condition, is in the main homogeneous. We find here no wealthy section, nor do we find a real 'slum district' to compare with it. Take then 4.6 as the average for the real family, and it is easy by comparison to note how some sections surpass, while others fall below this standard. The three sections which now lead the list for large families are nos. 8, 10 and 6, all with over five persons. On the other hand, the four localities where families are the smallest are 22, 13, 21 and 5, where an average of 4¼ persons per family is rarely exceeded. Between these extremes are ranged the other sections, but the order suggests little by way of a reason.

A comparison, however, of the figures of the several sections may cause us to modify some preconceived notions and may indicate, dimly shadowed, the working of certain natural laws which, though subject to constant exception, appear to operate in the main with tolerable regularity.

We are accustomed to say for example that certain nationalities, especially the French-Canadian, are remarkable for large families. This may be true in other parts of the city, but it does not seem to be so for the district now under study. The three sections, nos. 8, 10 and 6, which rank first in matter of large families are peopled in almost equal proportions by English, Irish and French-Canadians. Of the four sections which bring up the rear section 22 is mainly Irish, section 13 is four-fifths French, whilst in sections 21 and 5 the nationalities are nearly evenly divided. Again sections 17 to 20, immediately below Notre Dame street, show much larger families than do sections 12 to 15 just above it, yet all these sections are alike preponderatingly French-Canadian. The size of the family in this part of the city does not then appear to depend upon nationality.

We have also been accustomed to think that the poorer the locality the larger the family. The poor man's chief wealth is said to consist in abundance of children. Doubtless many individual instances may be cited in support of such an hypothesis but averages for a considerable number of families, at least in the district we are examining, tend to disprove this theory. Indeed, it is the contrary, rather that appears to be nearer the truth. Three out of four of the sections remarkable for the smallness of their family averages, are at the same time localities wherein the average family incomes are among the lowest to be found. Extremely low income seems an accompaniment of especially small families. The belt below Notre Dame street, where families are large, is a region of better average incomes and fewer poor than the belt above Notre Dame street, where the families are not large. Nor, on the other hand, does the family in the best sections, such as 1, 2, 3, 6 and 9, exceed the average size, sometimes even falling below it. Hence the law which appears to the writer to be dimly apparent is in effect that neither wealth nor poverty is likely on the whole to be accompanied by large average families. These are rather to be expected among the middle industrial class, and the average number of persons per household decreases as the social status of the residents rises above or falls below this level.

Another matter which invites examination is the adult element of the average family and its occupation. Our average family was found to contain 2.94 persons no longer children. Of these 1.41 work to support the family, while 1.53 are supported at home, where probably in most cases by the performance of household tasks they contribute their part. Here a law seems fairly apparent in that the proportion of wage-earners seems gradually to diminish and the proportion of home-tenders gradually to increase as one passes from an examination of the poorer to that of the more well-to-do sections. It is probably a fact that the poorer the locality, the greater the pressure to increase the number of contributors to the family purse, while the richer the locality the larger the number of those who may be allowed to remain at home.

As to the children, they are relatively most numerous in the sections below Notre Dame street and least numerous in those above St. Antoine street. As to the division into children of school age and infants, beyond noting the fact that the poorer the section the more nearly equal are these two portions, and the better the section the more the former exceeds the latter, we venture no conclusions.

The child element, in the typical family, we found to be expressed by the figures 1.64. In an examination, made in connection with this census, of 400 families among the very poor, this child average was exactly maintained. This fact furnishes additional corroboration of our claim that it is not among the very poor that the average number of children will exceed the standard.

It has been asked — 'Has information such as has just been presented any value other than as matter of sociological interest?' Its practical value appears to the writer to be this. Should the time come when capital shall be ready to be invested in the erection of improved industrial dwellings, it is evident that for its intelligent expenditure, in this or that locality, definite knowledge must be in hand as to the personnel and composition of the average family of the section selected. The number and size of the rooms to be provided, in the improved dwelling for the average family, will depend not only upon the size of the family, but also upon its composition, since the larger the proportion of the adult or school-child element the more the amount of space and air that will need to be allowed.

To make a success of this work of improvement we can afford to allow no facts to be overlooked. Hence this endeavor.

Chapter 4

Family incomes and workers' wages

The unity, yet separation, of these two topics / Explanation of map D / The family income, all classes included / How localities vary in this respect / The individual income, all classes included / Some noticeable variations / The minimum and where it is found / The 'real industrial class,' who compose it, how large it is / The family income in this stratum of society / The wage of the individual worker therein / An attempt at an average by sexes / Real value of this investigation

EXAMINATION into the question of the family income and the remuneration of the wage-earner, when resident within 'the city below the hill,' will form the subject of this, our fourth, sociological study. Although allied topics these two themes may best be considered separately and in the above order. With regard to each we will first survey the field as a whole, then consider the characteristics of certain localities and finally offer some suggestions regarding the utilization of information of this nature.

Let us turn first then to map D and familiarize ourselves with the meaning of its figures in order that comparative examination may become possible. Above the Roman characters, by which each section is designated, is the amount of the average family income therein per week, all classes included. Immediately below the Roman letters is the average weekly income per individual for all persons of the given section. To the left is shown, by percentages, the division of the residents of that section into three classes, viz.: above – the well-to-do; between – the real industrial class, and below – the poor. In this article it will be mainly the middle class of which we shall treat. The amount specified at the bottom is equivalent to the average weekly family income among the 'real industrial class'; while to the right is expressed the average weekly earnings per wage-worker among this same order. The meaning of these terms will become clearer as we proceed.

We have already learned that there are 7671 families resident within 'the city below the hill.' As near as can be ascertained these families receive, each week, an aggregate amount of not less than eighty-five thousand dollars. This means eleven dollars per week to each family. We have also found that these families include 37,652 persons. This gives, on an average, an allowance of two dollars and a quarter per week to each individual. *Eleven dollars per family, two and a quarter dollars per individual, these then are the standards of average living in 'the city below the hill.'*

Some sections exceed, while others fall below this limit of average income. Turning to the map and comparing the localities with one another, we note that, as a rule, the family income is highest in the group of sections north of St. James street. The average here for the ten sections, nos. 1 to 10, is $12.64, with only two sections, viz: 5 and 8 falling below this figure. Section 9 leads the list with an average of nearly $16.00 while sections 3, 6, 2, 7 and 4, in the order mentioned, complete the list of the six best sections within the entire nether city. Next in order of merit for generous incomes are the belts between Notre Dame and William streets, sections 16 to 20, where the average family income is $11.41, and below the canal, nos. 28 to 30, showing a combined average of $11.42. Then follows the strip between St. James and Notre Dame streets, sections 11 to 15, averaging $10.59. Finally there is that group lying between William street and the canal, where the lowest group average of $9.26 is to be found. There are six sections, with reference to belts, where the average family income falls below $10.00. There are nos. 12, 13, 24, 22, 21 and 23 with a range from $9.87 in the first to $8.03 in the last mentioned. As we shall see when we come to study 'poverty,' it is absence of the well-to-do and prevalence of the very poor which in these localities so reduce the average family income.

Two dollars and twenty-five cents, it will be remembered, was the amount determined upon as the average share per individual of the weekly income. Comparison of family with individual incomes brings out several noticeable facts. Arranging the sections in order of merit, the northern strip is still found as a whole to give the best average per person, but sections 1, 5 and 8 have slipped down towards the lower end of the list. Sections 12 and 13 make a better showing here than they did in the matter of the family incomes. Sections 21 to 24, however, still bring up the rear, and in these sections, comprising the major part of old 'Griffintown,' one dollar and seventy-five cents per week, *or twenty-five cents a day* is the amount upon which the average resident finds it necessary to live.

But this paper is to deal more especially with the real industrial class. It is then necessary that we determine who belong properly to this order. Among the families below the hill no less than 1176, or $15\frac{1}{3}$ per cent of the total number, were classified by the canvassers either in accord with their own information or because of their obviously comfortable surroundings as 'well-to-do,' that is in receipt of an average income of not less than $20.00 per week, or a thousand dollars a year. This number included proprietors, managers, professional men, store-keepers and a few families wherein the combined income of several workers yielded a generous income. It is plain, however, to to include these, together with their profits or salaries, when seeking to ascertain the income of the real industrial class would unduly elevate the figures. On the other hand there

FAMILY INCO

ABOVE = THE AVERAGE INCOME
FAMILY OF ALL WITHIN THE SEC
CENTRE = HOW MUCH PER HEAD OF
POPUL
BELOW = THE AVERAGE WEEKLY INC
OF THE INDUSTRIAL FAMILY.

Map D.
WORKERS WAGES

RIGHT = THE AVERAGE WAGE OF THE
INDUSTRIAL WORKER

LEFT = PERCENTAGE OF FAMILIES
BELONGING TO REAL INDUSTRIAL CLASS
ALSO WELL TO DO (ABOVE) AND POOR (BELOW)

were discovered by the canvassers families to the number of 888 which, for reasons to be studied later, were living upon incomes not exceeding five dollars per week. These latter familes and their meagre earnings should also be deducted from the original figures in order to prevent them from being unduly depressed by the presence of an element not properly belonging to the class now under study. The 'well-to-do' and the 'submerged tenth,' which together constitute twenty-seven per cent of the whole number, having been deducted, there remains 5607 families to be by us regarded as the real industrial class and as such examined. When then we ascertain that these 5607 families have an aggregate weekly income of $57,139.00, we conclude that $10.20 per family, or eighty cents less than the amount established as the average income when all classes were included, expresses the average weekly income among the real industrial class of the nether city. By way of further verification, were we to select the sixteen sections, designated by inner broken lines upon map D, wherein 75 per cent or more of the inhabitants are of the class in question, we would find that the average for these was $10.07. *From $10.00 to $10.25 per week, then, is the family income of the real industrial class.* As to variation on the part of the several localities from this standard, an examination of map D will make these apparent to such as care to pursue their researches further.

One final matter requires consideration before we abandon this subject. What is the average remuneration of the individual industrial wage-earner in 'the city below the hill'? The amount previously specified as receivable weekly by all the families of this class was earned by 7794 persons giving an average of $7.33 for the earnings of each worker. Taking only the sixteen typical industrial sections before referred to and submitting their figures to a similar test the result is $7.21, or twelve cents less. We are safe then in concluding that between $7.20, and $7.35 per week, or about *$1.20 per day, is the average wage per worker,* taking as a whole the real industrial class of the west end. We have not accurate data upon which to determine the approximate wage of the sexes, but since in our second paper we learned to expect to find in each group of wage-earners 20 per cent of them to be women, and 3 per cent to be children, this proportion being maintained, there would be, among the 7794 mixed workers, 6000 men, 1560 women, and 234 children.

If the men earned $8.25 per week, the women $4.50 per week, and the children $3.00 per week, it would account for the $57,139.00, the total amount earned by the aforesaid 7794 mixed workers. This estimate is but conjectural, yet it does not seem likely to be far wide of the mark.

This average per wage-earner of $7.33 is not maintained in all parts of the nether city. This is apparent by a glance at map D. In this calculation, however, it is the average for the largest number that is to us of most value and therefore we will not here call attention to the deviations in various sections. The study of poverty, yet to follow, will bring out local differences to better advantage.

We will not undertake a comparison of wages between Montreal and other cities. Nowhere else do I know of a study worked out upon exactly similar lines. We may be able, however, when the next Dominion census is taken, to compare results with results, and ascertain – what is of greater value – whether the number of the well-to-do is increasing, the number of poor diminishing, and whether the average wages of the real industrial class throughout 'the city below the hill' are advancing. If these conditions be then found present, we may consider that our city has truly prospered. The real measure of advance in any city is not the increase in the number of very wealthy men, nor of handsome residences, but in the improved condition of the middle industrial class. Increase in ability to surround themselves with influences which improve the mind, morals and health of this part of the community means elevation for society from its foundations, whereby all above is also raised. For signs of such advancement we will all watch with eagerness.

Chapter 5

The homes of the wage-earners

The theme outlined / What the ideal home should provide / map E explained and illustrated / 1 The number of persons per building and tenements per house here and elsewhere; advantages and disadvantages of the small house / 2 The rear tenement; its prevalence, the dangers arising from it and the way to secure its abolition / 3 The privy pit; where most numerous; how it may be caused to disappear; why there is no excuse for its continued presence / 4 The number of rooms in the average tenement; local variations; comparison with Glasgow / Conclusion: the difference between the average and the ideal home should constitute a summons to action

WE ARE now come to the point where investigation is necessary as to residential conditions in 'the city below the hill.' Before we can take up the study of comparative rentals we must know something regarding the differing accommodation which the several localities provide. We have then as our present task to answer a series of questions as these:

1 Does the industrial class of the west-end, as a rule, occupy lofty tenement houses or small dwellings?
2 Is any considerable portion of our people to be found in rear tenements?
3 What sanitary accommodation do the several localities provide?
4 How many rooms, on an average, constitute a home and how greatly does this number vary with different sections?

1 I think we will all agree that the ideal home is one where the front door is used by but one family, where the house faces upon a through street, where water-closet accommodation is provided, and where there are as many rooms allotted to a family as there are persons composing it. That this ideal is by no means universally attained goes without saying. By means of the accompanying map we can note how far the different localities fall short of this desired standard and, having thus acquainted ourselves with the extent of the deficiency of each we can more intelligently consider in our next article the matter of comparative rentals. A few words of explanation, however, are here necessary with regard to map E. The figures above the section number denote the average number of tenements per dwelling house. The percentage to the right indicates the relative proportion of front and rear tenements, the percentage to the left the proportionate sanitary equipment, while the figures below signify the average number of rooms to a family in the section under consideration. If, for example, we take section 1, the average number of tenements (families) to each residential building therein will be seen to be 1.46; of these tenements 89 per cent front on the street and 11 per cent on lanes or rear courts; of the occupied tenements 81 per cent are provided with water closets and 19 per cent with privies; while there are 6.28 rooms on an average for each family.

It may be of interest at the commencement of our enquiry to compare the number of persons per dwelling house, as ascertained for several large American cities, with our figures in this regard for the district under consideration. According to the United States census, the number of persons to a dwelling house in Philadelphia was 5.6, in Baltimore it was 6.2, in Chicago 8.6 and in New York 18.52. Taking into consideration the poor districts only in these same cities these figures were advanced in Philadelphia to 7.34 persons per dwelling house, in Baltimore to 7.71, in Chicago to 15.51, and in New York to 36.78. Now our 'city below the hill' can scarcely in fairness be contrasted with the former series of averages for it does not contain the usual proportion of larger residences occupied by single families, nor, on the other hand, can it be justly compared with the so-called 'poor districts' of the above cited cities; it would need then to be compared with a mean between the two series, and so, when the average dwelling house is found to contain eight persons, this figure proves that 'the city below the hill,' is rather one of small residential buildings like Philadelphia and Baltimore, than of lofty tenements like New York and Chicago. In fact, the average house throughout 'the city below the hill' accommodates two families, one being above the other below, as may be proven not only by observation but also by our special census which showed 4709 separate buildings to contain 8390 tenements, or on an average 1.78 per building. There is much variation between sections as to the number of tenements which the average house in each contains. The seven sections wherein this number is lowest, viz., nos. 4, 3, 2, 1, 5, 7 and 8, ranging from 1.25 to 1.58 – are all to be found above St. James street. On the other hand the seven sections, wherein the average number of tenements per building is the greatest – viz., nos. 12, 13, 14, 15, 18 and 20 – lie on both sides of Notre Dame street between Chaboillez square and the city limits. Nowhere, however, do we find a section averaging more than 2.15 tenements per building, the case in section 13. The fact that the wage-earner of western Montreal dwells in a small building is not without its effect upon him and his family. It tends to make him independent and self-reliant, preserving as it does all that pertains to separate family life. This state of affairs is without doubt more conducive to health and good morals than if the many were herded

C.P.R'Y

WOODST

100 % w.c.
0

1.81
IX

100 % F.
0   R.

ST. ANTOINE ST.

7.70

MARY ST.

DOMINION ST.

COURSOL ST.

80% w.c.
20% R.

1.73
X

5.53

97 %

F.
3% R.

GARLAW ST.

1.58
w.c.
70% VIII
30% R.

9%
F.
9%

6.05

MARTIN ST.

85% w.c.
15% P.

1.56
VII

6.40

SEIGNEURS ST.

1.58

90% F.
10% R.

LUSIGNAN ST.

1.71
VI

90% w.c.
10% P.

6.85

MT. ST.

AQUED

G.T.R'Y

CITY

49 % w.c.
51% P.

2.07
XV

4.28

89 % w.c.
11% P.

CANAL ST.

1.93
54% w.c. XIV
46% P.

86% F.
14% R.

4.76

49 % w.c.
51% P.

2.15
XIII

3.99

61% F.
39% R.

ST.   JAM

AQUEDUCT

NOTRE

BASIN

DRY DOCK

41% w.c.
59% P.

2.03
XX

4.60

93% F.
7% R.

SEIGNEURS ST.

61% w.c. XIX
39% P.

1.63

91% F.
9% R.

4.80

GUY ST.

53% w.c. XVIII
47% P

2.12

4.24

LIMIT

CANADA CORDAGE WORKS

LARARRE ST.

22 % w.c.
75 % P.

1.89
XXX

4.92

93% F.
7% R.

SHEARER ST.

BASIN

BASIN

40% w.c.
60%

1.83
XXIX

0.66

BASIN No 1

BASIN No 3

BASIN No 2

LACHINE   CANAL

90% F.
10% R.

CANAL ST.

STREET

39% w.c.
71% P.

1.71
XXVIII

4.21

93% F.
7% R.

BAS

CENTRE

ST.

STREET

WELL

G.T. RY
OFFICE

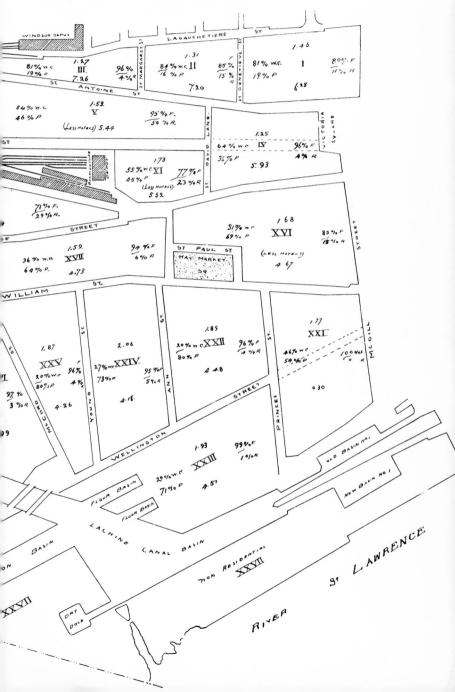

RIGHT = { ABOVE = PERCENTAGE OF TENEMENTS FRONTING ON STREETS
          BELOW   PERCENTAGE FRONTING ON LANDS AND IN REARS.

LEFT = { ABOVE = PERCENTAGE OF TENEMENTS WITH WATER-CLOSETS.
         BELOW = PERCENTAGE OF TENEMENTS HAVING PRIVIES.

together in huge caravansaries where privacy was impossible. There are also, however, some disadvantages. The small house means but few ratepayers per acre, and this on expensive land, means high rentals or mean accommodation for those who occupy. Small houses mean enhanced cost of heating, and since it is easier to inspect a limited number of large dwellings than many small ones, insanitary conditions are permitted to remain, in connection with small houses in out-of-the-way places, which would be noticed and abolished by the authorities did they exist on a larger scale. On the whole, however, I am inclined to regard the advantages of the small house, occupied by few families, as outweighing the disadvantages attendant upon this condition of living.

2 The second task set for us is to answer the query: Is any considerable proportion of our people to be found in rear tenements? It is somewhat difficult to define just what constitutes a rear tenement. Those buildings facing upon back yards or courts, to which entrance from the main street is by a covered passage or a narrow lane, where the buildings are so concealed by those in front as scarcely to be visible from the thoroughfare without, such are rear tenements without question. In our investigation, however, we have also come to regard many dwellings, facing upon a passage-way (perchance dignified by the title of 'Avenue' or 'Terrace'), so narrow and so remote from the street that the disadvantages of the rear tenement were all present, as entitled to be classed in the same category. Including such the total number of rear tenements discovered, in the course of our special census of the district, was 860 or an average, if evenly distributed, of about one in ten homes for every section. Certain sections – see map E – such as 13, 12 and 11, greatly exceed this average, the first with 39 per cent, the second with 29 per cent and the third 23 per cent of rear tenements. The neighboring sections to these in the same lateral belt, viz., 14 and 15, also exceed the average, as also do sections 1, 2 and 16. Section 9 is absolutely free from this evil, while sections 6 and 10 are nearly so. The presence of the rear tenement always renders a neighborhood less desirable for residence. It is not only bad in itself but it takes up the space, light and air which properly belong to the house in front of it. The rear tenement is rarely well built, and, being hidden from the public eye, is oftimes permitted to be occupied long after it has

fallen into such a state of decay that it is no longer fit for human habitation. If one desires to find where drunkenness and crime, disease and death, poverty and distress are most in evidence in western Montreal, he has only to search out the rear tenements. The typical rear tenement is either an ancient wooden cottage of the rural *habitant* type or a two-storey building encased in refuse bricks and reached by rickety wooden stairs and galleries. It is high time in Montreal that the majority of these hovels were condemned as unfit for habitation, and that our City Council were empowered by legislature to confiscate and demolish such as were not, within a reasonable period, torn down or removed by their owners. It is already within the power of the City Council to prevent the erection of further buildings of this type, and if we are to keep pace with the advanced municipalities of the old land we must go a step further and give to the civic authority, as representing the public welfare, the right to interfere even with what are known as private interests and vested rights, when these latter are, as in this case, a menace to the welfare of the community. The rear tenement must go.

3 We now come to a consideration of the sanitary accommodation to be found in 'the city below the hill.' It will doubtless be unexpected information to many of the citizens of the upper city — where such a thing is unknown — to learn that that relic of rural conditions, that insanitary abomination, the out-of-door-pit-in-the-ground privy, is still to be found in the densely populated heart of our city. That the privy pit is a danger to public health and morals needs no demonstration, and yet in 'the city below the hill' *more than half the households* are dependent entirely upon such accommodation. This evil is naturally greatest in the older residential quarters where many of the dwellings were erected before the day of proper drainage, and where the ideas of their owners, upon what constitutes proper accommodation for tenants, are as antiquated as their crumbling properties. There is a map in my office whereon are colored in yellow all blocks of buildings containing only proper sanitary accommodation, and whereon the presence of the privy abomination is designated by shades of purple from violet to nearly black according to its prevalence. The sections above St. Antoine street are upon this map mostly yellow. Between Mountain and Richmond streets this favorable color comes down as far as St.

James street. Beyond Canning street it again creeps down to Dominion avenue. This irregular strip and occasional faces along St. James and Notre Dame streets, are the only considerable patches of yellow color upon the entire map, are in fact the only neighborhoods of any extent throughout the nether city where water-closet accommodation is universal. Turning to map E we note that the belt composed of sections 1 to 10 contains but 22 per cent of privies, although 4 and 5 greatly exceed this average. Section 9 alone is wholly exempt, though section 6 is nearly so. The second belt, made up of sections 11 to 15, contains proper and improper sanitary accommodation in about equal proportion. The third belt, sections 16-20, is slightly inferior to its predecessor, only 44 per cent of the families here having water-closet privileges. It is reserved, however, for old Griffintown to surpass all other localities in unenviable pre-eminence in this regard. Throughout that belt (see sections 21 to 26 on map E) *only one family in four* have water-closet accommodation. In certain sections of it (such as 22, 25 and 26) the proportion with proper sanitary equipment is but one tenement in every five. Nor is there much improvement below the canal for the percentage of families using privies throughout sections 28 to 30 reaches 72 per cent. On this score then the localities above St. James street are most advanced in the process of ridding themselves of this evil, those sections bordering the canal and within the limits of Griffintown are most backward and in great need of attention and ameliorating effort.

The number of privies, throughout the entire city of Montreal, has considerably diminished during the past five years. Although there are to-day 3000 less of them than in 1891, the total number at the beginning of 1896 was still nearly 5800. It certainly does not seem to me that the work of eradicating this evil is being pushed forward with the energy and despatch which the urgency of the case demands. The evil is still so wide-spread and abundant that only drastic measures, born of persistent agitation, will suffice to extirpate it. It is now quite in order to prohibit the erection of further privies within the city limits, and it would not be going too far were our corporation to provide, by by-law, that, if, after a reasonable period had elapsed — say two or three years from date — any landlord within the city limits shall thereafter continue to be the owner of a privy, he shall be taxed for it at the rate of $10.00 per annum until he be thus forced to abate the same as a public nuisance. There is no excuse for permitting this evil longer to exist. There is not a street or lane in our nether city which has not a water service. Only a few small alleys are without a drainage system. Not one house in twenty could plead exemption upon this score. But even if a water-closet in every home is a thing as yet unattainable, we can at least where necessary adopt the Birmingham pail system, whereby all night-soil is collected and removed once in every twenty-four hours. Even this improvement would remove many of the most objectionable features of the privy pit as we know it. This much of an advance we might at least make. Would that Montreal might enter the twentieth century with this reform an accomplished fact.

4 Our last consideration in regard to the homes of the west-end is with reference to the number of rooms the average family occupies and how this number varies with different sections. The special industrial census, already so frequently referred to, showed that the 7671 families in 'the city below the hill' occupied 38,543 rooms. It will be seen that the average is a trifle over five (5.02) rooms per home. This indeed compares favorably with other cities. The best district in Glasgow averages but a trifle over four rooms per family. The locality which makes the best showing is section 9 which boasts 7¾ rooms for every family. The order of merit is then as follows: sections 9, 3, 2, 6, 1, 8, 4, 10, 11, 5, 19, 14, 17, 16, 29, 7, 20, 23, 22, 30, 12, 21, 15, 25, 18, 28, 24, 27, 13, 26.

It will be seen that, with the exception of no. 7, every section above St. James street shows an average of at least 5½ rooms per family. In fact, the combined average of sections 1-10 is over six rooms per family. This high average, however, does not characterize the remaining portion of 'the city below the hill.' Four and a half rooms per family seems elsewhere about the usual rule. In the belt between St. James and Notre Dame streets the average is 4½ rooms. In that belt which lies between Notre Dame and William streets it is $4\frac{3}{5}$ rooms. In old Griffintown it is $4\frac{3}{10}$, while across the canal it is $4\frac{2}{5}$ rooms. There are in all these sections a certain number of homes occupied by families hardly belonging to the real industrial class; probably if these were deducted from the calculation we would find the average home of the west-end industrual worker still to contain at least four rooms.

Dr. Russell, the head of the Glasgow Health Department, is responsible for the published statement that of every one hundred families in that city 30 per cent live in one room, 44 per cent in two rooms, 15 per cent in three rooms, and only 11 per cent in four rooms and upwards. How far superior are the conditions which we have been examining? This can be demonstrated by comparing with the above figures those of that section of the nether city most likely to approximate similar conditions. Take, therefore, section 13, where the average number of rooms reaches the lowest limit known to our limited experience – a little under four (3.99) rooms per family – and we find that in this section there is not a family living in a single room, but 14 per cent of the families having only two rooms, 31 per cent with three rooms, 31 per cent with four rooms, 9 per cent with five rooms, while 15 per cent with six rooms or more. The comparison is overwhelmingly in our favor.

And now we have about covered the ground set apart for the present study. If we could imagine ten average families coming to settle within 'the city below the hill' the division of accommodation among them may be expressed as follows: One family might secure an entire house to itself, but nine families must needs share theirs' with another. Nine families might dwell facing the street, but one would have to live in the rear. Five families might have proper sanitary accommodation, but as many more would have to put up with the pit privy. Three families might have six rooms, four families might have five rooms, while the homes of the remaining three would contain four rooms. This, then, represents the home average for the dwellers of the west-end. There is still need for much effort before the home *average* can be brought up to the standard of the home *ideal* set forth in the introduction to this article.

Chapter 6

Comparative rentals

What a rental map by blocks will show / A few generalizations /
map F and its explanation / The average rental for the typical home /
Variations according to situation / The belts compared / How
sanitary equipment affects rental values / What proportion rental
takes of income / Some instances of very low rentals / Recapitula-
tion / How to avoid the most common mistake of philanthropic
investment in workingmen's homes

IN OUR preceding article we considered the homes of 'the city below the hill.' We learned what the dwelling place of the average family offered by way of situation, sanitary convenience and room space. We noted also the local variations from the standard. We are now therefore prepared (1) to enter upon a consideration of the cost of such accommodation to the average family; (2) to examine how this amount varies according to the locality; (3) to consider certain other conditions which influence rental values, and, (4) to ascertain how large a proportion of his income the average wage-earner finds it necessary to set aside for rent.

A map of the district under examination hangs upon my study wall. It shows by graduated colors how rental values vary with every block. Where the average family rental for a block reaches or exceeds $20 per month a light lemon color is used; where the average falls below $5 per month a deep chocolate tint renders this fact apparent. From lemon to chocolate are nine shades of color, each representing a lower rental as the color deepens. A glance at this map suggests a few generalizations. It is noticeable that the bands of lighter color as a rule border the streets which run *the length* of our nether city. Lagauchetiere street shows a high rental average for that portion within the district. St. Antoine street, especially from Mountain street to the city limits, is also evidently lined with residences of the better class. St. James and Notre Dame streets, though occasionally showing a darker tint for a block or two, indicate a higher than ordinary rental average. It is upon streets running at right angles with these main thoroughfares that lower rentals predominate. The darkest spots of all, representing the lowest rentals, will be found upon short side streets, or blind alleys and in rear courts. Near the city limits these dark spots grow more frequent, but their presence here, as we shall see, is less ominous than when they occur in localities nearer to the city centre.

Map F, accompanying this article, regards our district as divided not into blocks, but into sections. It deals with averages obtained by grouping together a number of contiguous blocks. Consequently the higher rentals of the main thoroughfares are neutralized by those of the less frequented streets, giving a resultant not fairly representing either class, but still of value for purposes of general comparison. An explanation of this map is therefore next in order. Above the Roman letters, designating the number of the section, will be found the average rental throughout this group of blocks, together with the number of rooms which that sum will here procure. Below is the average rental value per room. To the left is indicated the grade of accommodation, estimated upon the proportion of families in every hundred that have water-closet accommodation. (Thus section 9, every dwelling therein being properly equipped, is graded at 100, while section 22, with but one properly equipped dwelling out of five, is rated at 20.) To the right is shown how large a proportion of the average family income is required to pay the rent. With these data before us we will take up our four points.

1 If the rental for every family of the 7671 within 'the city below the hill' were equal, the amount would be about $8.75 per month. In return for this sum, as we have seen, five rooms might be expected; there would be nine chances out of ten that the home would be upon an open street and one chance in two that it would contain proper sanitary conveniences. As this gives an average rental value of $1.75 per room, were a family to need only four rooms the rental should fall to $7.00, while for six rooms $10.50 would seem a reasonable charge. I am quite aware that averages, obtained by combining the figures of sections so different in character, are not of much real value, yet it is worth while noticing that for the real industrial sections these general estimates do not come very wide of the mark.

2 Great indeed is the variation from the average standard in this matter of rentals. For instance we have in section 3 an average rental almost reaching $16.00, while in section 26 it is but $6.30 per month. *Location* is a most important factor in determining rental values, and by grouping sections according to natural affinities we may measure the popular estimate of certain neighborhoods on this score. *(a)* Considering as a whole that group of sections which lies above St. James street, we find that here the highest amounts are paid for rent. Sections 1 to 10 combined show a rental average of $12.30 per dwelling or $1.94 per room. In sections 2, 3, 6 and 9, about $15.00 per month is the ruling figure, while only in sections 5 and 10 does the average rental fall below $10.00. Equally good accommodation is of higher cost in the northern than in the southern end of this belt. Thus, though only 81 per cent and

Map

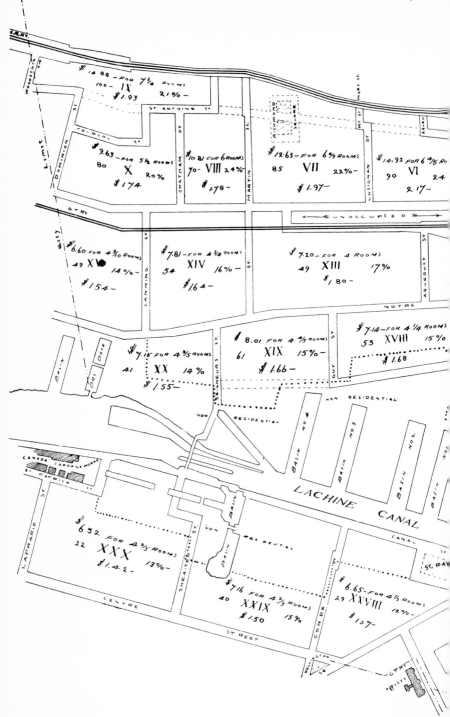

E = THE AVERAGE RENTAL FOR THE SECTION

W = " " " PER ROOM THEREIN

Y = PERCENTAGE WHICH RENTAL TAKES OF INCOME

EFT = GRADE OF ACCOMODATION

NDSOR DEPOT

LA GAUCHETIERE ST.

$15.92—FOR 7½ ROOMS
81 III 25%—
$2.19—

$15.01—FOR 7½ ROOMS
84 II 25%—
$2.08—

$12.11—FOR 6³/₁₀ ROOMS
81 I 24%
$1.92—

ST. ANTOINE ST.

$9.58—FOR 5²/₃ ROOMS
54 V 19%
$1.69—

(HOTELS)

JAMES ST.

$13.33—FOR 5⅔ ROOMS
64 IV 24%—
$2.24—

(HOTELY)
$11.12 FOR OR 6²/₃ ROOMS
55 XI 22%—
$1.74—

4 ⁴/₅ ROOMS
18%—

(HOTELS)

8.84—FOR 5³/₄ ROOMS
31 XVI 19%
$1.52—

STREET

$8.47—FOR 4¾ ROOMS
36 XVII 16%—
$1.79—

ST. PAUL ST.
HAY MARKET
SQUARE

ST.

$6.43 FOR 4¼ ROOMS
20 XXV 14%
$1.50—

$6.44—FOR 4⅓ ROOMS
27 XXIV 17%—
$1.54—

$7.11—FOR 4½ ROOMS
20 XXII 20%—
$1.58

$7.44—FOR 4³/₁₀ ROOMS
46 XXI 21%—
$1.73—

McGILL

FRANCES ST.

$6.70—FOR 4½ ROOMS 19%
29 XXIII $1.48

SIDENTIAL

FLOUR BASIN

LARGELY NON RESIDENTIAL

OLD BASIN NO1

NEW BASIN NO1

FLOUR BASIN

LACHINE CANAL BASIN

BASIN

XXVII

NON RESIDENTIAL

RIVER St LAWRENCE

XXVII

ONT DOCK

IDENTIAL

84 per cent of the dwellings in sections 2 and 3 have water-closet accommodation, while every residence in section 9 is suitably equipped, rents are proportionately higher near Windsor street than they are in the neighborhood of the city limits. *(b)* With the exception of sections 11 and 16 — which, because of the hotels they contain, do not present fair comparative averages — no section below St. James street exhibits a rental standard exceeding $8.50 per family. Taking that group of eight sections which lie between Chaboillez square and the city limits, nos. 12 to 15 and nos. 17 to 20, the average rental is slightly under $7.50 per family. As this is an industrial section *par excellence* this estimate may be taken as fairly indicating the average rental for families of the working class. *(c)* Between William street and the canal the average rental falls to $6.67 per family, though it is just possible that our figures hardly do this locality justice owing to the custom, somewhat prevalent, of paying lower rentals in winter and higher in summer. *(d)* Below the canal the rental average falls yet lower to $6.57, for this amount, however, more room space being here given than in 'Griffintown.' A room costs less in section 30 than anywhere else within our nether city. It may be laid down as a rule that the rental value per room will steadily decline as one draws away from the employing centres and towards the outskirts of the city. It is evident that the wage-earner who is blessed with a large family, and who can pay but moderate rent, withdraws to the suburbs where alone he can obtain the room space which his family demands. This, doubtless, accounts for the nightly exodus southward across the city line into Ste Cunegonde, noted in our second article.

3 But location and room space are not the only matters which affect rental values, the *character* of the accommodation also exerts upon them a great influence. It is difficult in this respect to compare the houses of one locality with those of another, but I know of no better method than to rank the sections according to the proportion of residences that they contain, having water-closet privileges; for this test can be fairly taken as indicative of the percentage of dwellings which are of recent and improved construction. It is by applying this test that we are enabled partially, at least, to explain the difference in rentals between such sections as 18 and 25. There is not much difference between them as to location. In both sections

4¼ rooms constitute the average home, yet this accommodation costs $7.14 in section 18, and $6.43 in section 25. The cause is apparent when it is noted that in the former section 53 per cent of the tenements have water-closets, while in the latter section this is true of but 20 per cent of the dwellings. Further comparisons may interest the reader. Take sections 13 and 26. Each supplies 4 rooms to the average family, but the cost per room in the former is $1.80, while it is but $1.57 in the latter. Now section 13 grades 49 points in sanitary accommodation, while section 26 is reckoned at only 19. By this fact the difference of rental value between them is in part at least accounted for. Again, contrast sections 12 and 30. The room average for each is 4⅖. A room in the former cost $1.79, in the latter $1.42. In sanitary accommodation section 12 is reckoned at 42 and section 30 at but 22 points. Both situation and accommodation here and in general influence rental values.

4 It is interesting to note what proportion rental takes of income, and how this proportion varies with different sections. Taking the district as a whole, 18 per cent of the total earnings, or nearly one dollar in every five, reaches the pocket of the landlord. In the better sections of the upper belt this percentage is exceeded. In sections 1, 2, 3, 4, 5, 6, 7, 8, 9 and 11 the proportion equals or exceeds 20 per cent. Between St. James street and the canal it will average about 16 per cent, the sections near McGill street considerably exceeding the figure, while those near the city limits falling below it. For the combined sections below the canal the average is but 13 per cent. Nowhere else in our district does rental take so small a proportion of income as beyond the canal.

The real industrial class cannot, as a rule, afford to pay more than 20 per cent of their wages for rent. It is among the well-to-do and among the very poor that a proportion higher than this will be most frequently found.

There were some surprisingly low rentals in certain quarters of limited extent within 'the city below the hill.' Five dollars a month for three or even four rooms in a rear tenement is not uncommon. When, however, in the district we are now considering, we find four dollars for three rooms or three dollars for two rooms — unless it be close to the city limits — we may be certain that the accommodation furnished is of the poorest quality. Yet even as low as $2 for two rooms was in several instances reported. One whole block, near the city limits, contained 57 families, each occupying three rooms, their average rental being but $4.33 per month.

In closing, let me re-state some of the more important conclusions which we have arrived at as a result of this study:

1 The average rental in 'the city below the hill' is $1.75 per month for each room, and since five rooms constitute the average home, our average family will pay $8.75 per month for rent.

2 Rental values are higher in the belt above St. James street than elsewhere throughout the nether city. The value per room gradually diminishes as one passes southward from McGill street and approaches the city limits. Rents in Ste Cunegonde and in St. Gabriel ward will be yet lower than in the districts we have examined.

3 Where location is of equal desirability the rental value will largely depend upon accommodation, and this may be best tested by ascertaining the sanitary equipment of the houses of the neighbourhood.

4 For the district, as a whole, the proportion which rental takes of income is 18 per cent. For families of the real industrial class 16 per cent is a fair average. Towards the city limits the proportion still further decreases. It is among the well-to-do and the very poor that rental is permitted to absorb from 20 to 25 per cent of earnings.

One of the mistakes most frequently made, in semi-philanthropic efforts to provide homes for working people, is the building of dwellings *too high priced* for the neighborhood. Incidentally this may benefit the locality, though only those already fairly well housed can take advantage of this better value. The bulk of the people live as before. In such experiments the first question should always be: what can the people of the district afford to pay? the next, what is the best value which philanthropic investment can furnish for this, the current price? These questions well considered in advance will minimize the risk of financial failure.

Chapter 7

Density and overcrowding

The difference in meaning of the terms / The three points to be considered: density, overcrowding and vacant property / 1 Density — Montreal compared with other cities; the western compared with other wards; 'the city below the hill,' its density; comparison of groups of sections; how this density should be relieved / 2 Overcrowding — the standard for the nether city; localities exceeding it; the densest regions compared; instances of overcrowding; a remedy proposed / 3 Amount of vacant residential property — various causes for lack of tenancy; the small percentage in working-class sections; proof that suitable dwellings for working people are not too numerous / Conclusion

DENSITY and overcrowding, by which we mean two entirely different matters, are to-day regarded by medical authorities as
exercising so great an influence upon public health that these subjects demand at our hands full and careful consideration. Density of
population is usually expressed in terms of persons to the acre.
Overcrowding has come to be regarded as referring to the number of
persons per occupied room. Were we to estimate the condition of a
neighborhood alone by the former test we might be drawn into quite
erroneous conclusions, since of two localities, having the same
density per acre, one may be occupied by three-storey dwellings
with abundant room space for all, while the other may be covered
with low-built hovels wherein the room space is wholly inadequate.
Evidently in such a case the former locality would be far less in need
of attention and reformatory efforts than the latter. Density and
overcrowding must therefore be considered together, and such is the
purpose of this article, while we will also deal, in conclusion, with a
third topic, viz.: the proportion of vacant residential property.

Let us first explain the accompanying map G to enable us, as it
were, to take inventory of the information at our disposal for a
comparative examination of the nether city upon these three points.
In each section the figures above the Roman letters show the total
population of the section, and the figures below the number of
persons per acre which this represents. This material will serve us for
a comparative study regarding density. The figures to the right
denote the number of rooms per family, those to the left the
number of persons per occupied room. This data will aid us when we
come to the study of the subject of overcrowding. Finally in the
lower right hand corner is to be found the proportion of tenements
that were found to be unrented in November last. These statistics
will assist us in determining whether there is a demand for additional
accommodation in the section indicated. By means of broken
diagonal lines the more thickly inhabited portions are indicated
upon the map, the greater the density the closer being these lines. A
dotted line marks off such portions as are non-residential, though
the space is still included in the calculation of the sections.

1 Having learned how to utilize the information set forth upon
the map, we are now prepared to take up the subject of *density*.
Judged by old-world standards, Montreal is not a densely peopled

city. It will average throughout its entire extent about forty persons to the acre. Neither are St. Antoine and St. Ann's wards – which are in part included within 'the city below the hill' – among the more densely populated of our city. While St. Louis ward averages 117 to the acre, St. James ward, 96; St. Lawrence, 67; St. Mary's, 63; and St. Jean Baptiste, 56; St. Antoine ward will only average about 47 and St. Ann's ward 35 persons to the acre. Our 'city below the hill,' which contains, over all, about 700 acres, a little over a square mile, averages about 55 to the acre and were the population evenly distributed could not be regarded as thickly inhabited. But when we deduct, as we reasonably may, the canal and wharves, the parks and streets, Bonaventure station and the non-residential section no. 27, we find a total population of 37,633 persons upon about 400 acres, or an average of 94 persons to the acre. This expression represents the density of 'the city below the hill.'

Taking one hundred persons per acre, as a standard by which to institute comparisons, we will examine the groups of sections which naturally make belts of territory. *(a)* Least densely populated of all is the belt made up of sections 28 to 30. Owing to the presence of numerous industrial establishments along or near the east bank of the canal, the residences here do not, as a rule, commence to appear until the second or third block back from it. Consequently for the territory between Centre street and the canal the population will not exceed 65 per acre, while the only locality more densely populated than the standard (having an average of 153 to the acre) is that situated between Shearer and Island streets. *(b)* No section throughout the belt between Notre Dame and William streets, sections 16 to 20, exceeds or even reaches a density of 100 per acre. Between Barré and Notre Dame streets there is a thickly peopled strip of limited extent averaging 160 to the acre; just below Chaboillez square lies a half acre on which reside no less than 174 persons; and the northern corner of section 20 exhibits a density of 190 per acre, but the rest of the territory in this belt does not exceed the adopted standard. *(c)* Below William street, however, throughout sections 22, 24 and 25, the average density exceeds the standard, reaching 120 per acre. But if one wishes to visit the most densely populated neighborhood in 'Griffintown' he will find it within the bounds of William, Colborne, Smith and McCord streets, where an average of 173 per acre is attained. The single block with highest record is that wherein is situated no. 6 Police station, where 498 persons occupy less than $2\frac{1}{3}$ acres, giving a density of 217 per acre. *(d)* The sections above St. James street, nos. 1 to 10, vary considerably but average 104 per acre taken as a whole. Sections 6, 8 and 10 show highest averages, with 140, 134 and 147 respectively. Section 11 appears to have a dense population, but the presence of several large hotels therein, with transient occupation, prevents us from being certain in our calculations regarding it.

(e) But it is in the zone known as the 'Swamp' that we find the greatest density. Sections 12 to 15, which contain about 54 acres upon which buildings have been or might be erected, have a joint population of 8863 souls, or an average throughout of 163 to the acre. Some areas of limited extent far exceed this belt average. Here are the most densely populated localities to be found in all the 'city below the hill.' One of these special districts lies below the railway track, between Mountain and Lusignan streets, where, in less than 10 acres, dwell two thousand people. Another densely populated locality stretches from St. Antoine to Notre Dame streets, between Richmond and Seigneurs streets. St. Martin street runs through the centre of it, and here a density of 230 per acre is reached. The densest block anywhere discovered within the nether city lies between St. Martin and Seigneurs streets, below the track, a blind alley called Leroux street traversing the middle of it. Here in a trifle over three acres can be found 955 persons, or *over 300 to the acre.* Think of it, a thousand people residing upon a space the size of one portion of Dominion square. If the residents of this block stood in a row, allowing about twenty inches to each person, they would form one solid line completely enclosing the block on its four sides. It becomes no longer a matter of surprise that upon election day, a single block in the southern corner of St. Antoine ward should be able to produce ten or even twenty times as many voters as an equal area above Sherbrooke street.

Two hundred persons per acre throughout any considerable extent of territory is not an average which can be permitted, in a city of small homes like Montreal, without special vigilance in regard to all that affects the public health. A district thus congested has demands upon the civic chest for expenditure upon ameliorating and preventative measures, not to be considered merely upon the basis of the proportion of taxation which it bears. With fifteen thousand of our fellow-citizens (between Mountain street and the city limits above Notre Dame street), having as their only breathing space scarcely an acre, called Richmond square, what more fitting way of celebrating the approaching anniversary of our noble Queen can be devised than to open and equip within this densely populated area a public park in dimensions and adornment worthy the occasion? Another means of relieving the congestion would be to extend Albert street, as homologated, from Bonaventure station to Canning street, opening a thoroughfare below the railway track. Something certainly should be done to give the residents of the 'Swamp' more breathing space.

2 The second phase of our question, the subject of *overcrowding* now claims brief consideration. This study deals with the matter of room space, and examines into the number of occupied rooms per family and per individual. As has been demonstrated, a section may show high density yet ample individual room space, so that the danger arising from the former cause may be neutralized by the latter condition. The number of occupied rooms throughout 'the city below the hill' is almost identical with the number of persons. In fact, the average would be about $1\frac{1}{50}$ rooms per individual. 'One person, one room,' may then be regarded as the standard. Where, as in sections 1 to 11, the average family accommodation exceeds five rooms, there are as a rule fewer persons than rooms. But where the home contains less than five rooms then more than one person is the average for each room. Two sections, such as 10 and 25, may rank when tested according to density nearly upon an equality, but when it is noted that in the former locality nine persons would have the use of ten rooms, while in the latter eleven persons would occupy the same number, it is evident that in the former section the congestion is far less dangerous than in the latter. When comparison was made between what are called 'Griffintown' and the 'Swamp' upon the matter of density, the latter was found to contain a considerably higher average per acre than the former. If, however, the two localities be tested by the number of rooms per individual which each allows, it will be found that while the 'Swamp' (sections 13 to 15) averages 1.08 souls per occupied room, the more thickly populated sections of 'Griffintown' (nos. 24 to 26) show an average of 1.13 persons per room. Evidences of overcrowding are more

apparent in 'Griffintown' than in the 'Swamp.' The locality which surpasses all others in the number of persons per occupied room is section 24, where a family of five persons will average but four rooms. We also noted that, as the city limits were approached, the density increased; the number of persons per room, however, generally grows less, so that the evil effects of the former condition are largely neutralized by the latter.

Instances ·of overcrowding were not infrequently discovered in the course of the industrial census, but their number was far less than had been expected. In less than two per cent of the families visited was an average of two persons per room reached, although cases, where five, six, seven or even eight persons were huddled together in two rooms, were discovered. Seven persons to three rooms was the condition of more than a score of families. Eight, nine, ten, or even eleven persons for three rooms; nine, ten and eleven persons for four rooms were found. The worst group of over-crowded homes was located on St. James street, just beyond Fulford, where 41 persons occupied 20 rooms. There is reason to believe that other parts of our city in this matter are greater trans-gressors than those we have studied, but for lack of data we can make no comparisons. The laws of health demand that in Montreal, as is already the case in Glasgow, overcrowding be prohibited by civic enactment.

3 The third and last point to be in this article considered is the proportion of vacant residences throughout our nether city and what is demonstrated thereby. Out of 8390 places of residence, 719, or about 8½ per cent were noted to be unrented and unoccupied in November last, when our census was made. This means one dwelling out of every twelve, and appears at first glance to be a large propor-tion. Local causes, however, accounted for lack of tenants in many cases. Thus, in section 2 it was uncertainty regarding the widening of St. Antoine street. In sections 7 and 8, where the vacant houses are nearly all above St. Antoine street, the vacancy was occasioned by their undesirable position, in that they were overshadowed by the C.P.R. track. Were it possible to deduct such residences as are tenant-less on account of similar local causes, such as were not erected with proper judgment in making the rental fit the locality, such as are very undesirable on account of extreme dilapidation – were it

possible to deduct these, it is probable that not 5 per cent or *not one house in every twenty,* would be unoccupied from other causes. Ordinarily it is in the well-to-do sections that the percentage of unrented dwellings will run highest; it is where the working people live that inoccupancy is less frequent. A score of blocks, in localities of the latter order, could be named wherein not a room is vacant. In the more thickly populated portions of the 'Swamp' and 'Griffin-town' only from 5 to 7 per cent of vacancy is the rule. When, as here, the number of persons desirous of residing within a given locality is so great that sixteen out of every seventeen available dwellings are regularly rented, it is quite reasonable to assume that were modern dwellings erected, carefully adapted to meet the needs and the incomes of the local inhabitants, such buildings would rarely, if ever, want for tenants.

In conclusion, we would affirm that 'the city below the hill,' as a whole, is not over populated. There is still much available land that might be built upon to accommodate that excess of wage-earners which, as we found in article II, now find homes outside. Certain densely inhabited localities are to be found, and such congestion should be relieved by the opening of new streets and parks. There does not appear to be great cause for alarm as to overcrowding – at least, not in this portion of Montreal – but even here cases are sufficiently frequent to demonstrate the necessity for regulations by the civic authorities upon this matter. It is well that we have learned the situation of the more densely peopled and more frequently over-crowded districts, in order that these localities may be watched with greatest care. The comparatively small percentage of unrented dwellings, among those suitable to the real industrial class, leads us to conclude that capital judiciously invested in providing homes for working people in 'the city below the hill' would be almost certain to earn reasonable dividends.

Map

DENSITY A...

ABOVE = TOTAL POPU...

BELOW = N° OF PE...

RIGHT = N° OF ROOMS...

LEFT = N° OF PERSO...

LOWER CORNER = PER...

RCROWDING

THE SECTION

R ACRE

MILY

CCUPIED ROOM

VACANT DWELLINGS

INDSOR DEPOT

LAGAUCHETIERE ST

ST ANTOINE ST

ST MARGARET ST

ST GENEVIEVE ST

VICTORIA SQUARE

6.28

1045
I
95

8%

645
II 7.20
87
14%

9/10

8/10

7.22
III
80
8%

7/10

7.26

1898
V 5.44
120
8%

9/10

JAMES ST

814
8/10 IV 5.93
72
5%

1115
8/10 XI 5.52
164
7%

ST DAVID LANE

BERT ST

4.39

9%

ST

1184
9/10 XVI 4.67
58
15%

RESIDENTIAL STREET

1327
1.04 XVII 4.73
94
11%

INSPECTOR ST

ST PAUL ST

HAY MARKET
59

DUKE ST

WILLIAM ST

2087
1.08 XXV 4.36
149
4%

1955
1.18 XXIV 4.18
113

1595
9/10 XXII 4.48
102
5%

ANN STREET

406
1.12 XXI 4.30
23

NON McGILL

7%

SMITH ST

YORK ST

COLBORNE ST

7%

646
1.05 XXIII 4.51
42
7%

PRINCES ST

WELLINGTON ST

OLD BASIN No 1

NEW BASIN No 1

6%

TIAL

FLOUR BASIN

FLOUR BASIN

NON RESIDENTIAL

LACHINE CANAL BASIN

BASIN

XXVII

NON RESIDENTIAL

RIVER St LAWRENCE

XXVII

DRY DOCK

RESIDENTIAL

Chapter 8

The poor of the west end

IT IS difficult to determine what shall constitute the low water mark of decent subsistence in our 'city below the hill.' Since a dollar a day is regarded as the minimum wage for an unskilled laborer, it would seem that $6.00 per week might be taken as the point below which comfort ends and poverty commences. But a dollar a day is by no means equivalent to $6.00 per week, since few are those, among this class of laborers, who can count upon regular work throughout the year. It is also an undeniable fact that there are frugal households, not a few, wherein $6.00 per week means independence and comfort. Below $5.00 per week, however, it is hardly possible for the weekly income to fall and yet permit of proper provision being made for a growing family, and although there are those who do this also, and all honor to such as can, yet we may safely fix the limit of decent subsistence at $5.00 per week and regard such families as, throughout the year, earn no more than $260.00, as properly to be termed 'the poor.'

Now that we have determined upon a standard of measurement, the first question to be asked the statistician of the 'city below the hill' is: How many families are there in this district that fall below the standard, in other words what is the extend of poverty? Of 7671 families, in the area under examination, 888 or $11\frac{3}{5}$ per cent stated in November last, in response to the inquiry of our canvassers, that their average weekly family income taking the year as a whole, did not exceed $5.00. This is then the 'submerged tenth' of western Montreal and its examination will form the subject of this article.

The accompanying map H is designed to furnish data for comparison along these lines. An explanation thereof is then of first necessity. The figures directly above the Roman letters represent the total number of poor families within the boundaries of the specified section. The figures directly below the Roman letters, signify the proportion of poor families within the boundaries of the specified section, that is the percentage of poor families therein. To the right is to be noted the percentage of families whose incomes are not regular throughout the year. To the left is shown the number of well-to-do families – whose incomes reach or exceed a thousand dollars a year – and below that again is the percentage of this class to the whole. By these figures we can ascertain the location and distribution of the poor, likewise of the well-to-do. We can also examine the relative proportion of irrregular incomes.

There are two sets of data furnished by map H for comparison between sections in respect to their poverty, viz: the numerical and the proportional statement. These, by no means, of necessity correspond. A district may contain but few poor families and yet, because thinly populated, may present a high poverty percentage. On the other hand a section wherein are many poor families, because densely populated, may not be prominent when ranked according to percentage only. In determining then what districts are of most unenviable pre-eminence as the *habitat* of poverty, attention must be paid to both the numerical and proportional statement.

The families of the poor are widely distributed throughout the city under the hill. We do not here, find them as in many other cities, grouped together in a locality with clearly determinable limits; on the contrary, but one of our residential sections, no. 9, contains none of this class among its inhabitants. The presence of the poor is not always apparent. Sections generally considered to be wholly consecrated to the well-to-do, contain, in out-of-the-way alleys and in rear tenements, a small proportion at least of needy families.

Two considerable areas, however, those indicated by broken lines upon the map, contain over half the poverty of the 'city below the hill.' These districts are 'Griffintown' and the 'Swamp.'

'Griffintown,' or rather that part of it which lies between William and Brennan streets, from Grey Nun to Young streets, is the home of nearly one thousand families, twenty-four per cent of whom, or *one out of every four, are living upon $5.00 per week or even less.* The four sections, nos. 21 to 24, included between these boundaries, contain 233 poor families or about one-fourth of the whole number resident within our nether city. No other district of equal extent can surpass this either in amount or proportion of poverty.

The 'Swamp' district, from Chaboillez square to the city limits, and between St. James and Notre Dame streets, comprising sections 12 to 15 upon our map, contains in all 1915 families, of whom 221 are 'poor.' Although the number nearly equals that in the previously described district, it will be seen that the poor families of the 'Swamp' constitute but 11½ per cent, or one-eighth part of the whole population, so that the proportion is only half as large as in 'Griffintown.' The two districts above described, when taken together, account for the location of more than half the poverty of the lower city.

Map

THE POOR OF THE W

ABOVE = NUMBER OF POOR FAMILIES.

BELOW = PERCENTAGE OF POOR FAM

RIGHT = PERCENTAGE OF FAMILIES WITH IRREGULAR INCOMES.

LEFT = NUMBER OF, OVER PERCENTAGE OF WELL-TO-DO FAMILIES

Two other sections, of considerable extent, may be further mentioned as containing more than the average proportion of poverty.
Section 16, which includes St. Maurice street, contains 40 poor
families about 17 per cent of the residential population, and section
8, owing to the rear tenements off St. Martin and Seigneurs streets,
also contains forty poor families or 15 per cent of those dwelling
therein. These two sections account for one-eleventh of the total
amount, and together with 'Griffintown' and the 'Swamp,' or ten
sections in all, leave but 354 poor families or only 40 per cent of the
poverty, to be distributed among the twenty sections that remain.

The two belts wherein poverty is of least frequent occurrence are:
that above St. Antoine street, where a large proportion of the residents are well-to-do, and that between Notre Dame and William
streets, south of Inspector, which includes the well-known Barré
street section, and is occupied almost exclusively by the real industrial class, with few among them falling below the standard. Section
9 alone, as previously stated, has no poor whatever.

It has often been affirmed regarding old 'Griffintown,' and similar
districts, that as soon as a family becomes well-to-do it moves to
another locality. That this is the case appears to be corroborated by
the evidence of our census. Barely one hundred families, or but 7 per
cent of the present residents of 'Griffintown,' have an income
exceeding $20 per week. Of this number fully one-half are grocers
and saloon-keepers whose business binds them to the locality. This
fact is unfortunate since it tends to reduce the general scale of living
by removing from a neighborhood such ameliorating influences as
can only be sustained where at least a fair proportion of the community are of the well-to-do class. In the 'Swamp,' sections 12 to 15,
eleven per cent of the families are of the $20 class, while in the belt
above St. James street 25 per cent belong to this order. In no other
district does one find so many poor and so few well-to-do as in
'Griffintown.' This region appears to have been by the latter class
abandoned to its fate.

As to the causes of poverty, chief among them is insufficient
employment. Few are the families where nothing is earned, although
there are such subsisting more or less worthily upon charity. Almost
without exception each family has its wage-earner, often more than
one, and upon the regularity with which the wage-earner secures
employment depends the scale of living for the family.

One of the matters investigated in our special census was this irregularity of work. Although as families in receipt of regular incomes were regarded such as possessed at least one worker employed without intermission, and also all families which receiving ten dollars or more per week for part of the year, might be reasonably expected to put aside sufficient to enable them to get through the remainder without hardship, yet even with these regarded as 'regular' there still remained 1724 families, or 23 per cent of the total number, whose small incomes could not be depended upon as constant and regular throughout the year. Of course this included many instances of alternative trades, as for example, when a man is a brick-layer in summer and a furnace-man in winter, but still the ratio of *nearly one family in every four without steady work,* seems alarmingly high and explains much of the poverty. The relative proportion of irregularity in employment varies greatly with the locality, but increases as one approaches the water front. In the belt above St. James street, the proportion is but one family in eight, between St. James and William streets it is one family in every five, beyond the canal it is one family in four, while between William street and the canal the proportion is *two* families out of every five. Think of it, of fifteen hundred families in all 'Griffintown,' six hundred do not know what it is to have a regular income and steady work. It is not at all improbable that these six hundred families could furnish nearly an equal number of able-bodied men to any local enterprise which, during the winter, would offer a living wage. With most of the wage-earners of these families the programme for the year is as follows: Work upon the wharves in summer and odd jobs of any sort during five long winter months. When spring arrives, overdue rent and debt at the corner grocery have so mortgaged the coming summer's earnings that saving becomes impossible. This irregularity of work is doubtless the main cause of poverty, for the prolonged idleness unfits many a man for steady work even when he at length succeeds in getting it. Once irregular always irregular is apt to be true, and irregularity, demoralization and poverty is the order of descent.

It may not be at this point out of place to consider briefly the liquor question in its bearing upon the subject under examination. Whether the sale of intoxicants is the cause of irregular employment and poverty, or whether idleness and want bring into being and maintain the liquor stores we will not attempt to decide. This fact is, however, apparent to the observer, that *wherever poverty and irregularity are most prevalent, there the opportunities for drunkenness are most frequent.* Throughout 'the city below the hill,' there are, all told, 105 licensed saloons and 87 liquor selling groceries. Of these, 28 saloons and 9 groceries are to be found in sections 3, 5 and 11, in close proximity to the Windsor and Bonaventure stations, where it is apparent that they are sustained more by the travelling public than by the residential population. These sections can then fairly be eliminated from the calculation, thus leaving 155 liquor stores to provide for the remaining 27 sections, which means on an average one for every 45 families or one for every 219 persons. This is an exact though startling average for the 'city below the hill.'

Turn now to an examination of the locality between William street and the canal, and what do we find in this regard? Where every fifth family is in poverty, where two out of every five families are but irregularly employed, the population sustains one licensed – and no one knows how many unlicensed – liquor store to every 33 families, or one for every 160 persons. Look now, by way of comparison before leaving this subject, at the district beyond the canal, sections 28 to 30, with a population similar in respect to nationality to that of 'Griffintown'. Here one liquor store is deemed sufficient for each group of fifty families, one for every 240 persons, and here also one finds but *half* the irregularity in employment, and but *two-fifths* the proportional amount of poverty existent in the 'Griffintown' district just across the canal. Let this stand as evidence sufficient that drink is inseparable from idleness and poverty and vice versa.

It will be remembered that, according to our industrial census, the total number of poor families was reckoned at 888 in 'the city below the hill.' Half of this number were by the writer selected as material for a second and more searching investigation, with a view of more fully examining the characteristics, conditions and causes of our west-end poverty. Four hundred and thirty-six families were sought for, and the first fact that was brought to the notice of the investigator was that 46 families, or 10½ per cent of the above number, had left their former abodes, within the two months between the first and second canvass, drawing attention to one of the sad features of poverty's lot, viz., the constant necessity to move on because of inability to satisfy the claims of the landlord. If this ratio were maintained, and each month saw 5 per cent of the poor evicted, in a year not half these families could be found at the former addresses.

A second fact, made apparent by the special investigation, was that our west-end poverty was not the result of recent immigration. Quite the reverse from what would have been the case in New York or Chicago, hardly a dozen families were discovered that had not been residents of the city for at least three years. The vast majority were old residents who had lived in Montreal for the greater part of their lives. The presence of poverty, then, in the nether city is not chargeable to any considerable influx of foreign elements.

In the case of 323 families inquiries were made as to the causes, assigned by the people themselves, for their indigent condition. With 109 families, or 34 per cent the reply was 'irregularity of work.' The wage-earners were not without vocations but their employment was intermittent and often work ceased altogether for considerable periods. With 87 families or 28 per cent the answer was that the wage-earners had no work whatever, nor did there seem to be any immediate prospect of getting any. With 27 families, or 9 per cent, old age had unfitted and with a like number sickness had prevented the worker from earning the requisite support. Out of these 323 families, among the poorest of the poor, 62 per cent claimed to be able to better their condition were employment regular and abundant. That a certain percentage of the answers given did not state the real facts of the case is quite probable. Few are the families that will admit to a stranger that drink, crime or voluntary idleness is the cause of their misery, though in 7 per cent of the cases visited drunkenness was clearly at the bottom of the trouble. Still it is the belief of the investigator that the undeserving among the poor form a far smaller proportion than is generally imagined.*

* The following clipping from *The Outlook* of May 8th, 1897, is of value for purposes of comparison:

'The American Statistical Association publishes the records of the Charity Organization Societies of New York, Baltimore, and six smaller cities respecting the cause of need among the families whose condition was investigated last year. In a

As to the composition of the family, out of 390 families, 8 were found wherein the head of the household was a widow, and 54 cases where the husband was too old or too ill to work, making in all 140 families, or 36 per cent of the whole, that might be called 'decapitated' family groups. In about two-thirds of the families, or in 64 per cent of the cases examined, there was an able-bodied man in the house, oftimes more than one, a man able to work and professing to be willing to do so. If these proportions may be taken as fairly indicating the average among the families of the poor, it is evident that at least one-third of them are in indigent circumstances through no fault of their own. Death or disease have so crippled the family group that it can no longer unaided keep up in the fierce struggle for subsistence. Charitable effort must come to the relief of such. With nearly two-thirds of the cases, however, it is not charity that is demanded but a chance to work. Were employment obtainable these families would soon be able to adopt a comfortable scale of living. If private enterprise does not furnish sufficient opportunity for willing men to provide for their families the absolute necessities of life, during the four cold winter months, then the municipality, by care-

condensed form the results reached were as followed:

Chief cause of need	New York Per cent	Baltimore Per cent	Smaller cities Per cent
Lack of employment	48	43	35
Sickness	18	18	17
Intemperance or shiftlessness	18	13	20
Miscellaneous causes	14	21	27

What is notable about this table is that in all these cities the want of employment was believed to be the cause of distress in as many cases as sickness, intemperance, and shiftlessness combined. This, too, it must be remembered, was among the families which applied to public charities for aid. Among those which have been aided by the trades-unions and by their own relatives, the proportion of those whose need was due to the want of regular work was doubtless much larger. One labor union in this city paid 'out-of-work benefit' to over one thousand families during the greater part of the recent winter.'

fully considered relief works conducted at a minimum wage, should come to their assistance.

Still another matter, examined into by the investigator, was the scale of living among these 'poor' families. Of 390 families visited, 19 per cent were classified as 'comfortable' even upon slender means; 40 per cent were regarded as 'poor but self-supporting,' that is to say, able to subsist without outside help; 30 per cent were considered as 'very poor' and likely to need aid before the winter ended; while 11 per cent were, without question, 'destitute' and requiring immediate charitable assistance. If this proportion be constant – and we have every reason to expect that it would be so throughout the unvisited balance of the 888 poor families – then there are in 'the city below the hill' nearly one hundred families in a condition of absolute destitution, while not less than 250 will need to be helped before the arrival of spring.* This is a conservative estimate, the actual destitution is probably greater, it can hardly be less.

By way of acquainting myself in a measure with what was being done through our various charitable institutions for the relief of the suffering poor, I sent to several of them a list containing the names and addresses of needy families belonging to that special race or creed which each society represented. I asked that the organization should indicate what names were already upon its relief roll. From the replies obtained I gathered that a very considerable proportion of the families known to me, were already being cared for by our charitable Boards. The House of Industry and the National Societies aided the needy Protestants. The St. Vincent de Paul Societies assisted the French-Canadian families in distress, especially the widows. The parish authorities seemed well acquainted with, and in many instances were assisting the worthy poor among the Irish Catholics. But besides these there are also many independent organizations, benevolently minded groups and sympathetic indi- viduals, all contributing to assist their suffering fellow-men. Evidences, however, are not lacking to prove that this benevolent work frequently overlaps with a tendency to pauperize the recip- ients. This is a result that should be guarded against with greatest care. I am strongly of the opinion that our great weakness in the

* This statement was prepared in February 1897.

work of assisting the worthy poor lies in lack of organized effort among the charitable bodies. Some Central Charity Board, upon which representatives of every race and creed might sit, should be here established. A joint roll should be kept. There should be a sort of clearing house in respect to relief effort, where every needy case could be assigned to the organization responsible for it and whereby a family already in receipt of help from one source should not be further assisted from others. There is in Montreal abundant willingness to help those who cannot help themselves, but it wants proper guidance and direction.

What now have we endeavored in this article to set forth on the subject of the poor of the west-end? With regard to the district as a whole we have shown who are the poor, how numerous they are, their location and their distribution. We have also indicated where poverty was most frequent and the proportion of well-to-do to be found in working class sections. As to causes we have considered irregularity of work, intemperance, decapitation and other factors, and, by a more careful study of a group of poor families, brought out certain characteristics and conditions. We have advocated municipal relief work for the able-bodied and charity organization in dealing with families incapable of self-support. Here then may properly be brought to a close the present article.

Chapter 9

The death rate

An accepted test of progress in sanitary science / It can be lowered / A high rate means unwholesome conditions / Comparative death rates, here and elsewhere / The rate for 'the city above' and for 'the city below the hill' / Comparison by belts in the nether city / The four localities with highest death rate / Summary of the conditions therein / Conclusion

'THE CLOSER people live to one another' says Dr. Russell of Glasgow, 'the shorter their lives are.' This statement needs no proof, for it is universally admitted that urban conditions are less conducive to general sound health and long life than rural surroundings. With natural conditions against the city, it is only by the exercise of additional precautions that this handicap can be overcome. Now the test to which the cities of the civilized world by common consent annually submit themselves, in order to determine how successful or otherwise each has been in the struggle against these natural disadvantages, is a determination of the local death rate. By means of a knowledge of the mortality of the municipality as a whole, a city can compare itself with its neighbors and thus note its relative advance along lines of sanitary science. By remarking what regions within its borders show a death rate higher than the ordinary, that city can ascertain the sections that are lagging behind and in need of special attention. Thus a high death rate for any city, or for any particular region within it, has come to be regarded as a danger signal, a finger of warning pointing to that locality and declaring that there must therein exist conditions detrimental to the public health, conditions which demand increased effort for their eradication or improvement. And since it has been, during the past quarter of a century, repeatedly proven, that the death rate can be materially lowered, can be even reduced by half, through the amelioration of local conditions, it gives us an added impulse for examination into the real state of our own case, in the hope that to know our deficiencies may be a step in the path towards their removal.

    In this article we purpose, after a few comparative figures, (1) to compare the death rate of 'the city above' with that of 'the city below the hill,' (2) to critically examine certain localities within the latter region which the test of high death rate brings into unenviable prominence and finally to review the conditions of life which, in previous articles, we found existent in those sections where the rate of mortality is high. For the entire Dominion, during the year 1893, fourteen persons out of every thousand was the proportion of deaths. In the Province of Quebec this was higher, viz., 19 to the thousand. During the same year about twenty-five (24.91) per thousand died within the limits of the city of Montreal. Quebec province exceeds the Dominion rate, and Montreal city shows a record less creditable than that of the province. In 1895, the last year for which the official record for the entire city is as yet obtainable, the death rate in Montreal was 24.81 to the thousand. Only twice before in our civic history has it been so low, and we may congratulate ourselves upon the fact that since 1873 our civic death rate has diminished no less than forty per cent. Yet compared with other cities we have as yet little cause for boasting. In 1894, the cities of London, Paris and Birmingham could show that they had reduced their death rate to 20, Rome had reduced hers to 19.4, and Brussels to 18.1. Boston in 1893 had a death rate of 24.02 and New York of 23.52 and a steady decrease in these cities is also apparent. What has been done elsewhere in the lowering of the death rate should also be possible for Montreal and a further reduction is expected and demanded.

Great are the variations of the several wards from the average death rate of Montreal. In St. Jean Baptiste ward the death rate for 1895 was 35.51 per thousand, in St. Mary's ward it was 33.20, in St. Gabriel ward it was 32.32. Compared with these localities, our 'city below the hill' does not present the alarming symptoms noticeable elsewhere. Our nether city is mainly made up of territory belonging to St. Antoine and St. Ann's wards, and of these the death rate for the former as a whole is but 18.13, and for the latter 16.83. Evidently the conditions for the locality which we have studied are not so severe upon human life as they are elsewhere, although even here we found many matters demanding improvement. Through the courtesy of the Civic Health Department I have been enabled to ascertain the number of deaths (not including those which occurred in hospitals, institutions and the like) which took place, during the year just closed, for each separate block within the 'city below the hill.' Having previously learned, through out industrial census, the population of every block, it became possible to determine, not only the death rate per block but also for every group of blocks or section. Map I, whereon the territory is divided into the same thirty sections with which we have become already familiar, shows the population for each' section and also the number of persons per thousand who died within its limits during the year just closed. Here we have material sufficient to afford many comparisons.

During the year 1896 there were 832 deaths recorded among a population of 37,021 (those in institutions being omitted) within 'the city below the hill,' giving for this district a death rate, exceeding that of either St. Antoine or St. Ann's wards, a rate of 22.47 per thousand. Though this rate does not equal that of the city at large,

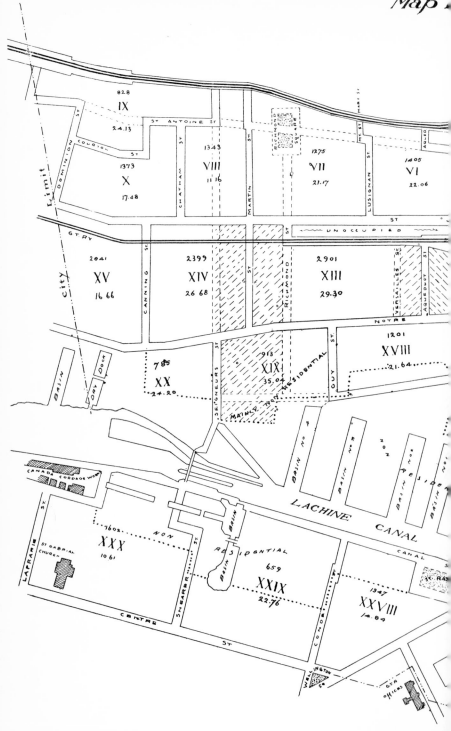

DEATH RATE (OMITTING INSTITUTIONS)

ABOVE = POPULATION

BELOW = DEATH RATE PER THOUSAND

DURING 1896

does not approach that of certain previously cited wards, it is still higher than need be, as may be shown by a comparison which we can make in this regard between 'the city below the hill' and 'the city above the hill.' St. Antoine ward, according to the health report of 1895, had a population of 50,607. It probably has to-day a larger population than this, in which case our contrast would be all the more startling. In that part of St. Antoine ward below the hill, reside, according to our census, 21,482 souls. Then above the hill about 30,000 persons will be found. Now the death rate for the whole ward is usually about 17 per thousand. But the death rate for that part which lies below the hill, sections 1 to 15, is 22¼ per thousand. It follows therefore that inasmuch as the rate for the lower portion of the ward is higher than the average, by so much will the rate for the upper portion of the ward be lower than the average. In fact, the rate for the 'city above the hill' will not exceed 13 per thousand. If then a rate as low as 13 per thousand has been reached for a locality in Montreal occupied by 30,000 people why cannot the same be obtained elsewhere?

But returning to our study of the lower city let us see if the average rate of 22.47 holds good throughout. This examination may best be conducted by belts. Sections 1 to 10 above St. James street show a rate of 19.75 per thousand; sections 11 to 15, between St. James and Notre Dame streets, a rate of 26.41 per thousand; sections 16 to 20, just below Notre Dame street, a rate of 23.32 per thousand; 'Griffintown' or sections 21 to 26, a rate of 24.62 per thousand; and the belt beyond the canal, sections 28 to 30, a rate of 14.41 per thousand. The most creditable showing is made beyond the canal and above St. James street, the most ominous indications are those of the 'Swamp' and of 'Griffintown.' The localities near the city limits, notwithstanding the density of their population, seem especially healthy and scarcely a block, beyond Seigneurs street, shows a death rate equal to the average.

I have chosen four districts, of limited extent, whose boundaries will not correspond with those of the sections with which we have grown familiar, but which present a local death rate so much above the average as to demand an examination into the attendant conditions. The first of these regions lies between Wellington, Grey Nun, Common and Brennan streets; the second between William, Young, Wellington and McCord streets; the third between St. James,

Richmond, Basin and Seigneurs streets; and the fourth between the Bonaventure station and track, Chaboillez square, Notre Dame and Versailles street. They are shown upon Map I by broken diagonal lines. Here are the mortality statistics for these localities together with certain data usually regarded as having an effect thereon. Along with these figures are given the average of our nether city, taken as a whole, in order that the differences may be apparent.

	Population	Number of deaths	Death rate per thousand	Density per acre	Persons per room	Percentage of 'rears'	Proportion of privies	Percentage of children under 5 years	Nationality
District 1	842	26	30.87	54	1.10	.05	67	10	Mixed
District 2	2087	65	31.15	149	1.08	.04	80	16	Irish
District 3	2532	86	33.96	170	1.09	.15	50	15	French Canadian
District 4	2179	84	38.54	134	1.10	.22	59	17	French Canadian
'The lower city'	37,021	832	22.47	94	1.02	.09¾	51	15	Mixed

Here we have a series of death rates, for groups of blocks, ranging from 30.87 to 38.54 per thousand. It would be quite possible to point out single blocks within these districts where the death rate last year greatly exceeded even these high figures, but with areas of such limited extent one can never be certain that he is not dealing with exceptional circumstances not likely to be repeated. In the above table, however, we have several districts, containing a population exceeding two thousand, a sufficient population to produce a stable average. In these four areas it will be noticed that in the matter of population per acre, persons to a room, proportion of rear dwellings and privy pits, these localities, almost without exception, fail to furnish accommodation up to the standard of 'the city below the hill.' This failure without doubt is in large measure responsible for the unusually high mortality which in these districts prevails. Until such conditions as are remediable, as for example the rear tenement and the privy, are legislated out of existence, and until such as are not wholly alterable, but which can yet be made less dangerous, are ameliorated, we, of this city, have still reason for agitation and effort. These four districts, and others like them, demand our special attention until their death rate shall no longer exceed the normal figure.

In conclusion I would again draw attention (1) to the fact that the death rate for 'the city below the hill' is far higher than it is for 'the city above the hill'; (2) that certain specified localities within our nether city, which combined contain one-fifth of its total population, exhibit a death rate *exceeding 34 persons to the thousand;* (3) that in these and other similar localities exist conditions which are undoubtedly responsible in great measure for this excessive death rate, and finally that these conditions can be improved and ought to be improved since thereby a saving of valuable lives may result.

Chapter 10

Nationalities and religions

General statistics / The nationalities of the 'Swamp' / Considering the nether city by belts / The three main elements of our population / The numerical strength and distribution of the foreign element / Some race characteristics noted / Figures relating to religious beliefs / Conclusion

AS previously stated, 'the city below the hill' has a mixed population. Considered as a whole, the 7670 families therein resident may be classified as follows: French-Canadian, 3218; Irish-Canadian, 2614; British-Canadian, 1596; all others, 242. Thus it will be seen that 42 per cent of the population (taken by families) is French-Canadian; 34 per cent is Irish-Canadian; 21 per cent is British-Canadian, and 3 per cent is of other nationalities.

That portion of the lower city which lies above Notre Dame street and belongs to St. Antoine ward is the home of 4307 families. Its population is thus divided: The French-Canadians number 2155 families or 50 per cent; the British-Canadians number 1079 families or 25 per cent; the Irish-Canadians number 916 families or 21 per cent, and other nationalities comprise 157 families or 4 per cent. Thus it will be seen that in this part of the ward the French-Canadians form one-half of the population, being equal to all other nationalities combined.

Grouping the sections into belts, as has been our custom in previous articles, we find that the strip of sections, nos. 1 to 10, lying above St. James street, has a population more evenly divided among the various nationalities than any other region. Of the 2183 families here resident, 791 or 36 per cent are British-Canadian; 659 or 30 per cent are Irish-Canadian; 628 or 29 per cent are French-Canadian, and 105 or 5 per cent belong to other nationalities. The British-Canadians have a majority in section no. 9 alone, as is indicated upon the map J by means of crossed diagonal lines. This element has a plurality in sections 2, 6, 7 and 8. The Irish-Canadians are nowhere in a majority but are in a plurality at the extremities of this strip, namely in sections 1 and 10, in each case not far from their parish church. The French-Canadians are nowhere in this belt in a majority though more numerous than any other nationality in sections 3, 4 and 5. Upon map J these variations can be noted, as the strongest element in each section is that for which the figures are placed over the Roman letters.

The strip between St. James and William streets, sections 11 to 20, through the centre of which runs Notre Dame street, contains 3217 families. Of this number 2190 or 68 per cent are French-Canadian; 510 or 16 per cent are Irish-Canadian, and 410 or 13 per cent are British-Canadian, with 107 families or 3 per cent of other nationalities. Here the French-Canadian is almost universally the predominating element. Only in section 11 does this nationality fall short of being more numerous than all the others combined, and although in sections 16 and 17 the majority is narrow, it soon becomes overwhelming as one passes to sections southward.

Between William street and the canal, sections 21 to 26, the Irish-Canadian is the most important element. Here are to be found 1517 families, of which 1047 or 69 per cent are of Irish extraction. The British-Canadian and French-Canadian elements are of nearly equal strength in this district, the former numbering 239 families, or 16 per cent of the resident population, the latter 215 families, or 14 per cent of the whole. Other elements here form but 1 per cent of the population. Sections 21 and 23 of this belt are but sparsely occupied by dwellings, only 220 families being found therein. Along Grey Nun and Common streets there is a considerable group of French-Canadian families. In fact, this element is the predominating one in section 21 and forms more than one-fifth of the population of 23. Elsewhere throughout 'Griffintown' the Irish-Canadians are in majority, the proportion steadily increasing as one approaches St. Ann's Parish Church.

Beyond the canal, sections 28 to 30, taken as a whole, show an Irish-Canadian majority over all others. The population here numbers 754 families. Of these 398 or 53 per cent are of Irish descent; 185 or 24 per cent of French extraction, and 156 or 21 per cent are British-Canadians. Only 15 families or 2 per cent may not be included among those three nationalities. It is to be noted that the French-Canadian element, with a strength of but 5 per cent in section 28, claims 24 per cent of the families in 29 and, in section 30 – which is partly in St. Gabriel ward – is the most powerful element, comprising here 41 per cent of the total number. Beyond Laprairie street, in that part of St. Gabriel ward which is west of the railway track, the French-Canadians are in the large majority.

Having dealt with the three main nationalities, let us now consider briefly the number and location of the foreign elements in 'the city below the hill.' These are here but 3 per cent of the total population, numbering in all only 242 families. Of these the German and Dutch number 94 families; Russian and Polish, 70; Negro, 24; Chinese, 18; Italian, 17; Scandinavian and Danish, 17; Spanish and

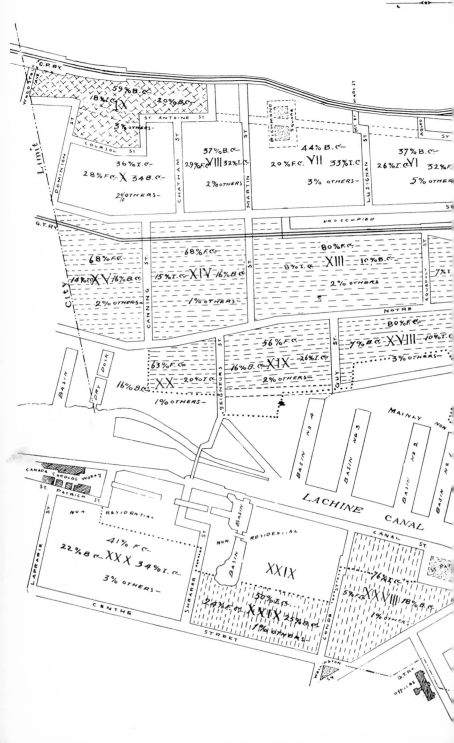

Map
NATIONALIT

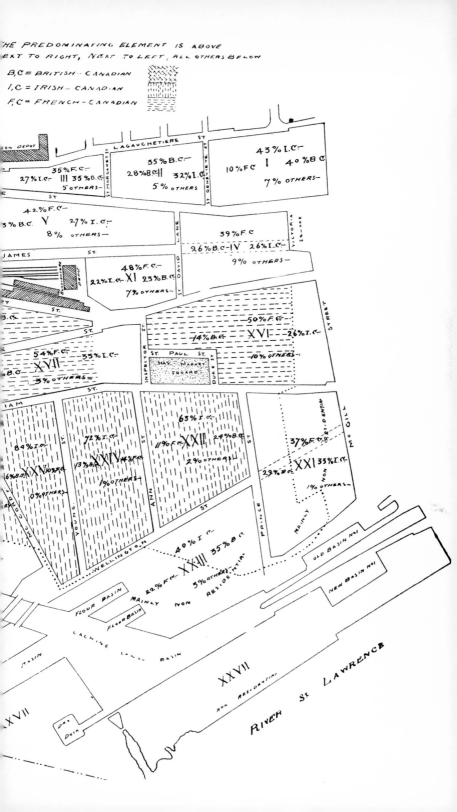

THE PREDOMINATING ELEMENT IS ABOVE
EXT TO RIGHT, NEXT TO LEFT, ALL OTHERS BELOW

B.C = BRITISH - CANADIAN
I.C = IRISH - CANADIAN
F.C = FRENCH - CANADIAN

Belgian one each. The Germans are to be found in almost every
section, especially along the avenues of trade. The Russians and
Poles, who are nearly all Jews, are found mainly along St. Maurice
street in section 16 and also in section 11. The negro element is
nowhere numerous, but is to be found in greatest number above
Bonaventure station in sections 5 and 6. The Chinese are mainly to
be found above St. James street. They have 14 laundries, a hotel and
a mission within the lower city and are usually located upon the
main streets. Owing to our inability to obtain definite information
regarding them, the Chinese have been generally omitted from previous calculations. There are but few Italian families; section 16
contains six, section 5 includes three and section 1 has two. The
Scandinavians are scattered. They have become, as a rule, merged
into the English Protestant element. In fact, the few families of
foreign lineage, within 'the city below the hill,' exclusive of the
Chinese cannot fail soon to be, if they are not already, so fully
identified with our native population as to be essentially Canadian.

Perhaps it may not be out of place, in view of the fact that we
possess considerable data regarding the various localities within the
lower city and now know the predominating nationality in each,
that we here turn our attention to a consideration of race characteristics to see if any such, through our series of articles, have been
made apparent. I trust I may offend no one in so doing and that it
will be borne in mind that I am not giving opinions but stating facts.
Let us, for purposes of such comparison, regard sections 12 to 20 as
the typical French-Canadian belt, since over two-thirds of the
families are of this race. These sections are shown by horizontal
broken lines on map J. The district made up of sections 21 to 30 we
will call the Irish-Canadian belt, as here two-thirds of the population
are of Irish descent, being indicated on the map by perpendicular
broken lines. Sections 1 to 11 we will call the 'mixed belt,' containing as it does the three elements in nearly equal proportions.
Section 9, the only section occupied in majority by British-
Canadians, is hardly of sufficient extent to be compared with the
other areas.

We have treated of many subjects in previous articles, we will see
how these three belts – The French-Canadian, the Irish-Canadian
and the 'mixed' belt – compare with each other upon these
matters.

The average size of the family (after deducting the lodgers)
in the 'Mixed' belt is 4.67 persons
in the Irish-Canadian belt is 4.57 persons
in the French-Canadian belt is 4.52 persons

The average number of wage-earners per family
in the Irish-Canadian belt is 1.43 persons
in the 'Mixed' belt is 1.41 persons
in the French-Canadian belt is 1.40 persons

The average number of home-tenders per family
in the 'Mixed' belt is 1.72 persons
in the French-Canadian belt is 1.48 persons
in the Irish-Canadian belt is 1.48 persons

The proportion of children under five years of age in the average family
of the French-Canadian belt is 16 per cent
of the Irish-Canadian belt is 16 per cent
of the 'Mixed' belt is 13 per cent

The percentage of school children in the average family
of the French-Canadian belt is 20 per cent
of the Irish-Canadian belt is 20 per cent
of the 'Mixed' belt is 16 per cent

The proportion of well-to-do families among the population
of the 'Mixed' belt is 26 per cent
of the French-Canadian belt is 12 per cent
of the Irish-Canadian belt is 9 per cent

The proportion of families belonging to the 'real industrial class'
in the French-Canadian belt is 77 per cent
in the Irish-Canadian belt is 74 per cent
in the 'Mixed' belt is 66 per cent

The proportion of regular and irregular incomes
in the 'Mixed' belt is 87 per cent reg. and 13 per cent irreg.
in the French-Canadian belt is 79 per cent reg. and 21 per cent irreg.
in the Irish-Canadian belt is 64 per cent reg. and 36 per cent irreg.

The proportion of families, living upon $5.00 per week or less,
among the total number
in the Irish-Canadian   belt is 17 per cent
in the French-Canadian   belt is 11 per cent
in the 'Mixed'   belt is 8 per cent

There is a marked difference between the several nationalities which
compose our population in ability to comfortably subsist upon very
small incomes. Of the poor families especially investigated, among
the French-Canadians 62 per cent were comfortable and independent even upon $5.00 per week, 58 per cent of the British-Canadians
were in similar condition, but only 51 per cent of the Irish-
Canadians of this grade were not in need of assistance.

The average family income for all classes
in the 'Mixed'   belt is $12.54; per individual $2.36
in the French-Canadian   belt is $10.73; per individual $2.27
in the Irish-Canadian   belt is $10.00; per individual $2.10

The average earnings per wage-earner
in the 'Mixed'   belt amount to $8.89 per week
in the French-Canadian   belt amount to $7.62 per week
in the Irish-Canadian   belt amount to $7.00 per week

The average family income of the 'real industrial class' only
in the 'Mixed'   belt is $10.92 per week
in the French-Canadian   belt is $ 9.92 per week
in the Irish-Canadian   belt is $ 9.87 per week

The average wage per worker among the 'real industrial class'
in the 'Mixed'   belt is $ 7.92 per week
in the French-Canadian   belt is $ 7.26 per week
in the Irish-Canadian   belt is $ 6.89 per week

The average number of rooms
in the 'Mixed'   belt is 6.13 per family
in the French-Canadian   belt is 4.50 per family
in the Irish-Canadian   belt is 4.33 per family

The average number of persons per occupied room
in the Irish-Canadian   belt is 1.09
in the French-Canadian   belt is 1.04
in the 'Mixed'   belt is .86

The average family rental
for the 'Mixed'   belt is $12.19 per month
for the French-Canadian   belt is $ 7.56 per month
for the Irish-Canadian   belt is $ 6.64 per month

The proportion which rental takes of income
in the 'Mixed'   belt is 24   per cent
in the French-Canadian   belt is 17½ per cent
in the Irish-Canadian   belt is 16   per cent

The average death rate
throughout the French-Canadian belt was 25 per thousand in 1896
throughout the Irish-Canadian   belt was 21 per thousand in 1896
throughout the 'Mixed'   belt was 18 per thousand in 1896

As to the sale of intoxicants.   In the
Irish-Canadian belt there are 26 saloons and 34 liquor groceries, or
    one liquor shop for every 179 persons.   In the
'Mixed' belt are 40 saloons and 24 liquor groceries, or 1 liquor shop
    for every 198 persons.   In the
French-Canadian belt are 39 saloons and 29 liquor groceries, or 1
    liquor shop for every 208 persons.

On the whole the 'mixed' belt, from these comparisons, makes the
best showing. Incomes and wages, rentals and accommodation, are
all upon a better scale there than elsewhere. The size of the family
and the proportion of the elements which compose it are very nearly
the same in the French-Canadian and in the Irish-Canadian belts.
Among the French-Canadians is to be found the largest proportion
of families belonging to the 'real industrial class.' For density and
high death rate the French-Canadians take undesirable precedence;
for overcrowding and poverty the Irish-Canadian sections make the
least creditable showing. Upon other points the comparison between

these two belts is, as a rule, more favorable to the former than to the latter nationality.

It has frequently been asked why a location in 'Griffintown' should be selected as the spot upon which should first be tried in Montreal the experiment of philanthropic investment in the form of improved dwellings for the working classes. I think the foregoing comparisons have already given the answer. It is because in this region the need at the present time is greater than in any other locality within our nether city, and because if success can be here attained it will be certain elsewhere.

In closing this article, the figures of our census respecting the religious beliefs of the families in 'the city below the hill' may also be given without comment.

Belt I sections 1-10 contain 1237 Roman Catholic families, 893 Protestant, 41 Jew, 11 Pagan.
Belt II sections 11-15 contain 1790 Roman Catholic families, 302 Protestant, 31 Jew, 1 Pagan.
Belt III sections 16-20 contain 915 Roman Catholic families, 135 Protestant, 42 Jew, 1 Pagan.
Belt IV sections 21-26 contain 1229 Roman Catholic families, 285 Protestant, 1 Jew, 1 Pagan.
Belt V sections 27-30 contain 600 Roman Catholic families, 152 Protestant, 0 Jew, 2 Pagan.

By the above it will be seen that 75¼ per cent of the families of 'the city below the hill' are Roman Catholic, 23 per cent are Protestant, .01½ per cent are Jewish, and about .00⅕ per cent are Pagan. Except in Belt I, where 41 per cent are Protestant, this element nowhere exceeds one-fifth of the population. Belt II contains 14 per cent, Belt III 12 per cent, Belt IV 18 per cent and Belt V 20 per cent of families belonging to the Protestant faith.

I trust that a fuller knowledge of 'the city below the hill' may result in the putting forth of more earnest and effective efforts for the improvement of this district.

This investigation has necessarily dealt with but a limited portion of our city, it has considered the case of barely one-sixth of our population. If, however, besides calling attention to certain local deficiencies the publication of this series of articles shall have accomplished anything by way of impressing upon the main body of our citizens the immense importance of collecting and interpreting similar figures for the city as a whole, my main object shall have been attained. It is unwise, even if it were possible, for private enterprise to undertake duties properly belonging to the municipality or the State. It is the duty of our civic and provincial authorities to secure for us similar data with respect to the entire city. By means of our civic servants, in the Police and Fire Departments and at the City Hall, a civic census could be annually taken within at most three days time. The task of obtaining accurate sociological statistics might be accomplished with less haste by our Assessors in connection with their regular annual rounds, or should a special department be required, an annual expenditure of a sum not exceeding $5000 would suffice to secure this much needed information.

Were we by such means enabled each year to accurately determine what progress was being made in improving the general condition of society, were we able every twelve months to place the finger upon every district which exhibited unhealthy symptoms, I have faith to believe that our citizens would not be unwilling to take the necessary steps towards betterment.

SECTION	Area in Acres, exclusive of Streets, &c.	Places of Employment.	Number Employed.	Men.	Women.	Children.	"Labor Units."	Places of Residence.	Number of Tenements.	Front Tenements.	Rear Tenements.	Occupied Tenements.	Vacant Tenements.	Occupied Tenements with Waterclosets.	With Privies.	Total Number of Rooms in Occupied Tenements.	Aggregate Monthly Rental.	Number of Families.	Number of Persons.	
			EMPLOYMENT.					RESIDENCE.												
1	11.0	60	1.698	1.235	454	9	1.465	135	198	177	21	181	17	145	36	1.137	$2.192	181	1.045	
2	7.4	15	947	242	668	37	586	92	121	103	18	104	17	87	17	749	1.562	104	645	
3	9.0	42	231	160	35	36	195	114	145	139	6	134	11	108	26	974	2.134	134	722	
4	11.3	163	1.264	1.054	191	19	1.154	132	166	159	7	157	9	101	56	931	2.094	157	814	
5	15.7	90	457	398	57	2	427	244	375	357	18	344	31	186	158	1.941	3.297	344	1.898	1
6	10.0	13	75	75	..	..	75	163	279	277	2	262	17	237	25	1.796	3.910	262	1.405	
7	16.0	21	96	75	21	..	85	192	301	271	30	259	42	221	38	1.658	3.272	259	1.275	
8	10.0	26	147	106	40	1	126	178	283	257	26	253	30	177	76	1.533	2.736	253	1.343	
9	11.2	3	3	3	..	..	3	114	207	207	..	178	29	178	..	1.372	2.650	178	828	
10	11.0	31	84	80	4	..	82	193	334	325	9	311	23	250	61	1.721	2.997	311	1.626	1
11	6.8	69	675	587	86	2	630	129	224	172	52	209	15	114	95	1.335	2.325	200	1.115	
12	10.0	42	130	108	22	..	119	172	334	297	37	301	33	125	176	1.322	2.38c	301	1.425	
13	19.6	41	180	169	11	..	175	328	706	428	278	661	45	325	336	2.639	4.763	661	2.901	1
14	14.7	52	157	142	15	..	150	276	534	461	73	496	38	266	230	2.364	3.877	496	2.399	1
15	9.5	49	76	57	19	..	67	244	506	452	54	457	49	223	234	1.956	3.013	457	2.041	1
16	20.4	151	1.957	1.227	717	13	1.588	158	267	227	40	227	40	70	157	1.312	2.007	227	1.184	
17	14.0	79	379	296	82	1	338	188	299	282	17	267	32	95	172	1.264	2.262	267	1 327	
18	12.5	51	173	141	32	..	157	125	266	248	18	249	17	131	118	1.057	1.778	249	1.201	
19	14.3	35	557	495	42	20	526	130	212	192	20	193	19	118	75	927	1.546	193	913	
20	14.5	38	631	483	148	..	557	88	180	168	12	157	23	65	92	722	1.123	157	785	
21	17.4	47	1.372	1.187	177	8	1.278	54	96	96	..	84	12	38	45	362	625	83	406	
22	15.5	29	647	476	146	23	562	197	374	358	16	356	18	72	285	1.597	2.533	356	1.595	1
23	15.5	42	633	625	8	..	629	76	147	146	1	136	11	40	96	614	912	136	646	
24	17.3	24	173	165	8	..	169	205	424	403	21	394	30	105	289	1.648	2.540	394	1.955	1
25	14.0	50	119	97	22	..	108	260	480	459	21	450	30	90	360	1.917	2.896	450	2.087	1
26	28.5	22	324	299	8	17	309	56	101	98	3	97	4	18	79	387	612	97	444	
27	50.0	23	1.050	915	..	135	950	3	3	3	..	3	..	1	2	12	15	3	19	
28	12.4	45	385	257	128	..	321	183	313	291	22	284	29	82	202	1.197	1.891	284	1.347	
29	21.8	39	1.103	995	58	50	1.041	80	147	133	14	131	16	53	78	610	938	131	659	
30	23.4	50	514	362	67	85	417	200	368	344	24	336	32	75	261	1.489	2.125	336	1.602	1
TOTALS	456	1.442	16.237	12.511	3.266	460	14.289	4.709	8.390	7.530	860	7.671	719	3.796	3.875	38.543	$67.005	7.670	37.652	

Tenders.	Number of School Age Children.	Number of Children 5 Years and under.	Number of Lodgers.	Aggregate Weekly Family Income.	Families with Income Regularly Received.	Families with Income Irregularly Received.	Number of Well-to-do Families.	Number of Industrial Class Families.	Number of Poor Families.	British-Canadian Families.	Irish-Canadian.	French-Canadian.	Other Nationalities.	Roman Catholic Families.	Protestant Families.	Jewish Families.	Pagan Families.	Number of Saloons.	Number of Liquor Grocers.	Number of Churches.	Number of Schools.	Number of Benevolent Institutions.	Number of Fire and Police Stations.	Death Rate per 1000 in 1896.
94	151	131	212	$2.130	130	51	44	108	29	73	77	19	12	100	74	7	..	4	4	2	..	..	..	18.18
66	102	78	175	1.462	84	20	43	49	12	37	33	29	5	65	34	3	1	..	1	..	2	..	..	23.16
45	106	60	144	2.100	126	8	70	60	4	45	35	47	7	82	48	2	2	6	1	..	..	..	3	20.77
38	144	91	123	2.024	126	31	58	82	17	41	41	61	14	99	49	8	1	6	1	..	..	..	..	25.79
01	226	244	481	3.796	319	25	55	269	20	79	92	143	30	232	97	13	2	10	6	1	3	2	..	19.58
80	253	204	78	3.777	251	11	84	165	13	98	68	83	13	144	113	5	..	..	1	2	1	..	..	22.06
42	225	151	58	3.400	232	27	74	261	24	113	87	50	9	127	128	2	2	..	1	2	1	1	..	21.17
96	243	184	23	2.663	203	50	20	193	40	93	82	72	6	151	100	1	1	2	3	..	..	..	..	11.16
52	160	90	8	2.840	177	1	66	112	..	105	32	36	5	60	116	..	2	..	..	2	..	..	..	24 13
78	310	244	25	3.412	263	48	25	249	37	107	112	88	4	177	134	..	..	..	4	..	..	..	..	17.48
25	160	126	216	2.404	175	34	53	138	18	48	45	100	16	144	53	12	..	12	2	1	..	..	F} P}	17.73
48	246	252	69	2.972	229	72	30	231	40	21	21	250	9	275	20	6	..	1	5	..	1	1	..	40.70
80	576	459	76	6.286	518	143	52	422	87	68	55	527	11	587	67	7	..	..	5	..	2	..	..	29.30
14	494	322	100	5.651	406	90	80	368	48	77	74	338	7	413	80	3	..	6	4	2	..	..	F} P}	26.68
40	404	354	25	4.901	358	99	47	364	46	74	62	312	9	371	82	3	1	3	5	..	1	..	..	16.66
35	195	174	164	2.397	165	62	44	143	40	24	60	111	32	180	22	25	..	10	3	..	..	..	..	22.12
79	293	218	55	3.250	239	28	42	217	8	25	87	146	9	231	28	7	1	7	2	..	..	..	..	17.33
92	25	212	28	2.659	189	60	31	190	28	16	26	198	9	222	18	9	.	7	1	..	..	..	..	21.64
98	146	158	26	2.307	160	33	28	162	3	31	50	109	3	154	38	1	..	2	2	..	..	..	..	35.04
52	160	123	23	1.867	129	28	19	135	3	26	30	99	2	128	29	..	..	3	2	..	1	..	..	24 20
29	73	71	35	681	44	39	5	63	16	24	27	31	1	59	24	..	..	3	1	..	..	..	..	44 34
24	263	271	67	2.920	222	134	8	270	78	86	224	40	6	242	113	..	1	9	6	1	1	..	..	21.31
18	118	58	34	1.093	84	52	7	94	35	48	55	29	4	85	51	..	..	2	1	1	..	..	F	23.22
67	436	359	50	3.442	218	176	25	265	104	51	284	55	4	337	56	1	..	..	11	..	2	..	P	19.95
30	382	346	57	4.857	265	185	51	355	44	26	377	47	..	414	36	..	..	3	8	..	..	..	..	31.15
34	87	66	15	1.065	67	30	11	71	15	4	80	13	..	92	4	..	..	1	1	1	..	..	..	10.91
5	5	4	..	38	3	..	..	..	..	..	1	2	..	3	..	..	..	..	..	..	..	..	..	..
98	275	189	46	3.468	224	60	40	221	23	50	216	15	3	233	50	..	1	3	3	..	..	..	..	14.84
94	146	110	21	1.459	93	38	23	93	15	33	65	31	2	98	32	..	1	3	1	..	..	..	..	22.76
66	316	264	44	3.677	247	89	41	254	41	73	116	137	10	266	70	..	..	3	2	2	..	..	..	10.61
11.720	6.948	5.053	2.478	$84.998	5.946	1.724	1.176	5.604	888	1.596	2.614	3.218	242	5.771	1.767	115	16	105	87	17	16	7	3 F 3 P	Average— 22.47 per 1000

The housing of the working classes

A lecture delivered on November 22, 1897

IT WILL BE necessary for me at the outset to define what I mean by the term 'the working classes.' We will seek our answer by means of a process of exclusion. All families that are rich or comfortably well-to-do, that is all households wherein the annual family income exceeds or equals one thousand dollars, I would not regard as properly belonging to the working classes. So also the submerged tenth of society, 'the dependents, defectives and delinquents,' those who have fallen below the level of decent subsistence, who could not, without outside help, survive through the rigors of a Canadian winter, such would I also exclude. These latter are fit subjects for state care and for charitable effort, and do not come within the limits of the present study. Between these two extremes, however, with a regular weekly family income from six to eighteen dollars, are what may properly be termed 'the real industrial classes.' These families, who probably number 4-5th of our total population, are 'the working classes' whose home conditions we are to consider.

The present inquiry then is one which deals with the material, physical and moral welfare of two hundred thousand of our fellow-citizens. Does not the obligation rest upon us to acquire, regarding these, that knowledge which will enable us to estimate, at least in some measure, our duty towards them?

The universal tendency of the present day is towards the concentrating of large numbers of persons in urban communities. Instead of decreasing, this tendency is certain to grow stronger in years to come. The cry 'to the towns' overwhelms the counter-cry 'back to the land.' We must be prepared for larger cities in the future than the world's history has ever known in the past.

Now, it is an admitted fact of sanitary science, that 'the closer people live together the shorter their lives are.' For conditions of perfect healthfulness, a certain amount of earth, air and water is requisite. These gifts of nature, man defiles in the using. If, as on the farm, this defilement does not too heavily tax the renovating power of nature, no serious result ensues. When, however, as is the case in a large city, people are compelled to live so near to each other that this natural recuperative power cannot make good the loss, *then* there is *danger* and unless sanitary science steps in to prevent it, sickness and death become ever increasingly frequent.

I wish it were possible to demonstrate, by means of statistical evidence dealing with our city as a whole, the truth of the theory just enunciated. Had we before us the figures of an accurate industrial census, such a census as has been prosecuted by many a continental city and by not a few in America, we could readily determine average conditions and place the finger upon the exact localities where human life, where the family of the industrial worker, is fighting against unjust odds. But although for the city as a *whole* such figures are lacking, yet there is a *portion* of it concerning which I *can* speak with a considerable degree of accuracy from the results of private investigation, and I believe that the conditions found there to exist will not differ materially from those elsewhere, and may therefore be taken as fairly typical of industrial Montreal.

The district I refer to is that which has come to be called 'The City below the Hill.'

As that locality within which most of us reside may be called 'The City *above* the Hill,' because it occupies the higher terraces and plateaus lying along the base of the Mount Royal, *so* that district below Lagauchetiere street and the C.P.R. track may by way of contrast be termed 'The City *below* the Hill,' inasmuch as it is nearly parallel with the river and in the main not over fifty feet above its level. Within Lagauchetiere, Centre and McGill streets and the city limits live nearly forty thousand persons. Within a square mile of extent, or about one-ninth of the total city area, is to be found one-sixth of its population. These people belong for the most part to the real industrial classes, and their homes will supply the material for our present examination.

SOME MARKED CONTRASTS

While you walk the streets of the upper city, you see tall and handsome houses, stately churches and well-built schools, but descend the hill, by Cathedral, Mountain, Guy or Seigneurs streets, and these characteristics change, the tenement house replaces the single residence, and the factory with its smoking chimney is in evidence on every side.

In other respects, at first glance perhaps not quite so apparent, the contrast between these two districts is still more marked.

DENSITY

In the *upper* city there are not more than fifty persons to the acre of extent, the *lower* city will average one hundred persons per acre throughout its entire occupied area.

In a single block on Young street dwell 500 souls.

Between St. Martin and Lusignan streets, within ten acres, live 2000 persons; between Mountain and Seigneurs streets, below the track, 955 human beings are crowded into a trifle over three acres.

Think of it, a thousand persons living on an area but slightly larger than the upper part of Dominion square. If the residents of this block stood in a line, allowing twenty inches to each person, they would form a solid row completely enclosing the block on its four sides. Or let us express this condition in another way. In the part of the city familiar to us were the land divided equally among its inhabitants, each person would be entitled to about 100 square yards as his share. If every person so provided stood in the centre of his plot of ground he would be about thirty feet from his next neighbor. But if he lived in this last mentioned block, but 12 feet instead of 30 would intervene. Or yet again. The average city lot above accommodates three persons, in this block that lot would be required to accommodate at least nineteen persons. I have multiplied illustrations for it is very important that you should fully realize what a density of 300 persons to the acre means. In this locality there are regions of considerable extent containing twenty times the population per acre to be found above Sherbrooke street.

SITUATION OF THE HOME

Again as to the situation of the home in respect to light and air, what is shown by comparison?

In the upper city the streets are wide, well paved and fairly clean. The houses, almost without exception, front upon thoroughfares. Not so in the lower city. Here one home out of every ten is situated either on a short narrow lane, in a bottle-necked court or directly in the rear of buildings which shut out the street. Out of every one hundred homes, in the district known as the 'Swamp' (sections XII, XIII and XIV on maps) thirty-two are of this character. In section XIII two homes out of every five are off the main street. The typical rear tenement is either a small two-story building encased with refuse bricks and in a tumbled-down condition, or else a wooden building of the rural *habitant* type, a relic of half a century ago. It is hard to determine which of these is the more objectionable. Both should be candidates for speedy extinction.

SANITARY CONDITIONS

What shall I say regarding sanitary equipment?

Upon this topic I find it difficult to speak with moderation. The sanitary accommodation of 'the city below the hill' is a disgrace to any nineteenth century city on this or any other continent. I presume there is hardly a house in all the upper city without modern plumbing, and yet in the lower city not less than *half* the homes have indoor water-closet privileges. In 'Griffintown' *only one home in four* is suitably equipped, beyond the canal it is but little better. Our city by-law prohibits the erection of further out-door closets, but it contains no provision for eradicating those already in use. With sewers in almost every street, no excuse for permitting this state of affairs to continue now exists, except it lies in neglect and in greed. On this topic I hesitate to speak further, but let any of you ask your family physician, or some other practitioner who visits below the hill, and he will tell you what are the effects on health and on morals, in the inclement weather, in the sweltering summer, of the out-of-door-closet within a crowded community.

BREATHING PLACES

In 'the city above the hill' are noble parks and numerous breathing places. Mount Royal is close at hand. By contrast look at this section, which lies between Mountain street and the city limits, extending from C.P.R. track to Notre Dame street. Here dwell 15,000 people, 5000 of whom are children. One paltry plot of ground, scarce an acre in extent, dignified by the title of Richmond square, is the only spot where green grass can be seen free of charge in all that district. I am far from being in favor of granting to corporations or individuals any of our city parks, but I would be willing to exchange some civic property not actually needed for an acre of land within the 'Swamp' to be converted into a park for the relief of this congested district.

After such marked contrasts in the matter of density, of situation, of sanitary equipment and of breathing places, between the city *above* and the city *below,* shall we be surprised if we find that the natural law enunciated at the outset of this paper, be found to operate with relentless force?

THE DEATH RATE

The local death rate is the accepted test, here and elsewhere, of the extent of deficiency that may exist in the matter of home conditions and surroundings. After what we have learned by comparison, we are not surprised to find that the death rate in the city *above* is 12 to the thousand, the rate in the city *below* is 22½ to the thousand. In more than half the cases the victims are little children. About one-fifth of the deaths in 1895 were due to typhoid and diptheria. Certain localities below the hill show symptoms indeed alarming. Between Versailles street and Chaboillez square is a region with a death rate of 40 per thousand. This is the city birth rate. It means that here as much life is consumed as is produced.

Between Richmond and Seigneurs streets it is 35 to the thousand.

Between Young and McCord streets it is 31 to the thousand. These areas we found to be all densely populated, now we find them also to be districts of death.

Can any of the conditions, you ask, which we have come to believe are causes contributing to produce high death rates in certain localities – Can any of these conditions be improved? We shall see. Take the first – Density.

Now, there are employed in 'the city below the hill' more than 16,000 persons, capable of supporting and who probably do support a population of 56,000 souls. But less than 40,000 persons now live within the district. Already about 17,000 of those nourished by the district, have to find homes outside the district. We can scarce then expect the population to decrease but rather the contrary.

The industrial class, in many cases must, in most cases prefer to live near their work. Even our cheap and rapid tram-car service does not materially relieve the strain. Add thirty-eight cents a week, or $1.60 per month, the price of transportation to and from work, to the cost of rent and you have a deterrent at once. No, we cannot hope to reduce the density. Our industrial population will and *must* live closely packed together, and the pertinent question for us to consider is: *How can the evil effects of this necessary condition be reduced to the minimum?*

By wise sanitary laws, faithfully enforced, the city of Birmingham, in which fifty years ago the rate of mortality was 30 to the thousand, has reduced that rate to 20 to the thousand. The city of Glasgow, with double our density, which, twenty years ago, showed also a death rate of 30, has now reduced it to 23½. The authorities of this latter city possess a minute knowledge of their people. Their census contains full and accurate information so they have been able, under the most adverse conditions, to bring about excellent results.

To lower the death rate of our city, which was 24.81 in 1895, by a single point would mean an annual saving of 250 valuable lives. To reduce our rate to that of Birmingham would mean 1200 persons added annually to our numbers.

The density we cannot alter, but with the rear tenement, the out-of-door-closet, the lack of breathing spaces we can deal more hopefully. These contributing cause of death can be rendered less potent and thus can be saved both life and character.

In this reform there are two sources to which we may look for aid — the state and the philanthropic individual. The first can coerce, the second can invite, together they can abolish. We want an enlightened public sentiment that will force our city authorities to drive out the rear tenement, to abolish the out-of-door-closet, to open up breathing places where needed. No tenement should be henceforth erected that does not face a thirty foot passage-way. Any dwelling in a condition unfit for human habitation, or so situated as to be deficient in the matter of light and air, should be demolished by order of the civic authorities and suffered to be rebuilt only in conformity with modern regulations. Where landlords refuse to demolish, I would give the state the power of confiscation, nor would I be chary in using such prerogative. Every landlord in the city, too, should be made to understand that if he will not, of his own free will, within a reasonable delay, abolish the out-of-door-closet, he shall be taxed for the right to maintain the abomination at a rate that will make the privilege rank as a luxury.

But I intimated that I was of the opinion that there was another way of assisting this cause besides legislation, and that was by philanthropic example. It is not by choice that the industrial classes — I do not speak of the submerged tenth, but of the self-respecting workingmen — occupy inferior quarters. They would not thus live were it possible to do otherwise. In the thickly populated sections of 'Griffintown' and the 'Swamp,' only about one house out of every twenty is unoccupied and many a block contains not a vacant room. Houses suitable for the requirements of the workingman, and at a rental which he can afford to pay, are rarely tenantless, that is for any considerable period. Many inferior dwellings find occupants only because all the better quarters at the same figure are already taken.

I am not an advocate for experiments in housing and lodging on the part of our civic authorities. They have no right to take chances

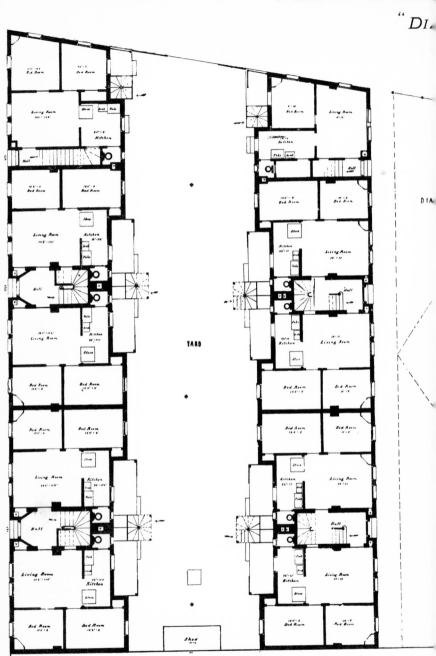

SCALE—ABOUT 19 FEET TO AN INCH

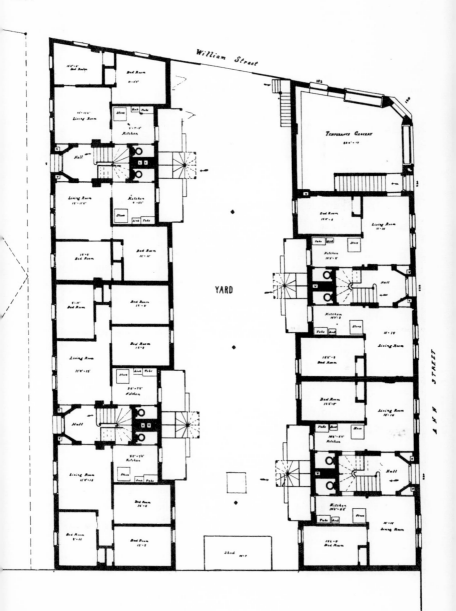

with the peoples' money. But here the philanthrope may well step in, and even at the risk of investing a few thousands at a comparatively low rate of remuneration, it is his privilege to show what can be done, and by experience to learn how best to do it. Every sanitary dwelling erected empties a rookery. There is a general moving up all along the line. Not only those who occupy, but a whole neighborhood, is benefited whenever a model dwelling is built therein.

Examples are numerous in other cities of 'Philanthropy and 5 per cent' united. The New York Society for the Improvement of the Condition of the Poor has, for the past fifteen years, never failed to pay a 5 per cent dividend.

Prof. E. R. L. Gould investigated 49 enterprises of this character in the old world and found 88 per cent of them to be financially a success.

A pleasing instance of faith in this idea comes from New York. When last year The City and Suburban Homes Co. was organized, it was a woman, Mrs. A. C. Clark, who stood responsible for half the money required for the first model tenement.

Undertakings of this character, however, can only succeed when the needs of the special city and of the particular district selected, have been first carefully studied. There are certain requirements varying with different localities, which must be fulfilled before the experiment will find approval among those for whom it is intended. We cannot expect to alter well-established preferences, but we should conform to the spirit of the district whenever possible without detriment. So it is well for us to stop here long enough to examine the type of family and of home among the working class in western Montreal.

The average family within 'the city below the hill' contains 4.9 persons. To every third family there is assignable one lodger. Deducting this element, which does not properly form part of the family, we have an average or typical family of 4.6 persons. In this family 1.41 work for wages outside the home and are the family's support; 1.53 are adults at home and may be called 'home-tenders'; 1.64 expresses the proportion of children, of which .91 is of school age and .73 an infant in the house.

These proportions may be expressed more graphically if we imagine a block to contain thirty average families. We would find

147 persons. Each morning 42, male and female, would go out to their work; later on 27 children would leave for school, 46 persons of adult age would remain to tend the home, 22 infants would be in the house, and there would be ten lodgers.

The home of the industrial worker of the nether city is not as in New York, a lofty building. There it is no uncommon thing to find 15 families with 75 or 80 persons in a single tenement house. The 'Big Flat' on Mott street, shelters nearly 500 people under a single roof. With us the small house is the rule. The typical dwelling, occupied by the industrial class, contains two families, the one above the other. Three-storey tenement buildings are rare, and then usually the two upper floors are tenanted by the same family This is the Birmingham rather than the London plan, and is possible only where land is not as yet too expensive. It has its advantages in that it tends to privacy and the conservation of those things which make for separate family life. But it forms constant temptation to land owners, especially of small properties, to cover over their land too closely with buildings, hence the rear tenement.

The industrial home of western Montreal contains on an average five rooms. Above St. James street 5½ is the rule. For the remainder of the nether city 4½ is the average. Were ten typical families, such as I have previously described, to settle in our nether city, we should expect to find one family taking seven, two families six, four families five, two families four, and one family three rooms. How different from Glasgow where half the homes of the city contain two rooms or less. Our people have set a good standard for themselves, and insufficient room space is not a common occurence.

The lowest room average we are acquainted with is in section XIII, and shows slightly less than four rooms per family. Here 706 households are thus accommodated. There are here no homes of one room. 14 per cent have only two rooms; 31 per cent have three; 31 per cent have four; 9 per cent have five and 15 per cent have six rooms and more.

On an average also there is but one person to each room. The number of persons and of occupied rooms in the nether city is almost identical. Section XXIV shows the highest average, with five persons to every four rooms. Though instances of overcrowding can be found, still not more than one home in fifty will have, what is for

Glasgow an average, that is two persons per occupied room. 'One person, one room' is the demand and the fact.

The rentals which our working people can, and do pay, are not exorbitant. They are much lower here than in other chief cities upon this continent, though higher than in Great Britain. For a home of six rooms or less, the cost will average about $1.75 per room. This means $5.25 per month for three rooms, $7.00 for four, $8.75 for five and $10.50 for six rooms. $8.75 is the average per month taking into account all the families of 'the city below the hill.' Above St. James street $10.00 to $15.00 rates rule, below this line $6.00 to $9.00 per month are the figures well-nigh universal.

In 'the city below the hill' as a whole, rental absorbs 18 per cent of earnings, although the well-to-do and the very poor oftentimes expend 25 per cent of their incomes on rent. It is not so with the real industrial class. From these latter the landlord receives usually from 15 to 20 per cent of earnings, and since about $10 per week is the average family income of the industrial class, so from $7.00 to $9.00 per month for a home of four or five rooms is what the family of this order generally requires.

Such facts as these, concerning the size of the average family, the nature of the dwelling preferred, the number of rooms required, the proportion of apartments of each size in demand, the rents which a neighborhood can pay, are all matters which must be known in advance if it be expected that a building experiment should prove popular among those for whose benefit it is intended. Now I come to this question:

Can *model* accommodation, such as will suit the pre-conceived notions of these people, and will, at the same time, conform to all the requirements of health – can such accommodation be furnished in Montreal with reasonable hope of a fair return upon capital thus invested? In reply I may be pardoned if I describe somewhat in detail my own experiment in this regard, even though it has as yet scarce emerged from the chrysalis stage.

Two years ago I purchased, at about eighty cents a foot, a piece of land upon the south-east side of William street, (between Ann and Shannon streets) in the heart of the district under study. For density of population, high death rate, overcrowding, general unsanitary condition and poverty, this locality was pre-eminent. Upon this piece of land now stand four blocks of buildings, containing homes of varying size and rental, for 39 families, with a grocery store upon the corner where no liquor is sold. The buildings conform to the popular type of small houses, three blocks being of two, and one block of three stories. The construction is of the most substantial character. The walls are of solid brick; the floors rest on steel beams and an air space in the roof gives warmth in winter and coolness in summer. The floors of the kitchen are of concrete and drain to the centre. There are ten three-roomed apartments for small families; twenty-two four-roomed apartments for the ordinary family of the neighborhood; four five-roomed apartments for larger families, and three two-storey six-roomed houses for foremen and similar tenants. The room will average 100 feet superficies and 900 cubic feet of space. The entries are lighted with gas, at the expense of the owner. The higher priced dwellings can have gas fixtures and slot meters. Each three-roomed and four-roomed house is supplied with a substantial cooking stove. Every dwelling has its own sink, stationary wash tub and water closet. There is a janitor on the premises, his services being given in lieu of rent.

Between the two inner blocks is a court 30 feet wide with an electric light and a garden of flowers. Between the backs of paralled blocks the yards are concreted and are washed with a hose once a week by the janitor. Separate clothes-drying apparatus is supplied to each family. Each tenant has his own garbage can, and twice every week the contents are removed during the night. In the rear are two vacant places for the children, not very inviting it is true, but with swing and sand heaps and such high surrounding fences that the bairns can be found when wanted.

For this the tenants pay as follows: 3 rooms at $1.50 to $1.75 per week, 4 rooms at $2.00 per week, 5 rooms at $2.50 per week, 6 rooms at $11.00 to $12.00 per month.

These rates include gas in the entries, water, janitors' attendance, etc. were such items deducted, the charge for rent would be about the same as the average of the neighborhood, while the grade of accommodation is infinitely superior. An agent is employed to collect all rentals and any family that pays regularly throughout the year, is allowed two week's free occupation during April. So far the houses have rented readily and seem to meet the needs of the locality.

I believe that this undertaking when once fairly running will yield five per cent on the investment, it has already yielded much by way of satisfaction.

Few realize the opportunity of the landlord to come into touch with the daily life of his tenants. Miss Octavia Hill and her associates in London, Mrs. Miles and others in New York, have grasped this idea, and upon it founded their system of friendly rent collecting, thus securing an entrance into many a workingman's home and being able to become adviser, helper and friend.

The erection of dwellings, such as have been just described, elsewhere through 'the city below the hill' is greatly needed. With land at eighty cent a foot, as on William street, it is impossible to furnish the workingman of large family with a five-roomed house such as he ought to have at say $7.50 per month, which is the utmost that he, out of his $1.25 a day, can afford to pay. In section XXX, however, he could be given what he needs for that figure. There are sections in our nether city, notably, XII, XIII and XIV, which cry aloud for model dwellings. Here the people are densely packed, but with model dwellings, such as are described, they could live just as closely together and that without danger to health.

The 'Diamond Court' dwellings will, when fully occupied, contain at least 160 persons upon half an acre of land, and yet a healthier community it is difficult to find.

Had we the results of an industrial census for all Montreal, we would discover other localities, especially in the eastern half of our city, equally worthy of attention, but I should advise no investment until the conditions of a neighborhood could be thoroughly studied.

We cannot interfere with the inscrutable law of supply and demand to raise the workingman's wages. We may feel, I know I do, that the pittance for which many toilers slave is far from sufficient or right. But wages will ever rest at the mark just above the requirements of absolute subsistence. We can, however, aid in making the workingman's hard-earned dollar bring him the fullest return, we can assist in making it possible for him to secure for himself a place fit to be called a home wherein he may bring up his children in health, in privacy and in comfort. To this end scientific knowledge and business experience are both requisite.

I desire your co-operation, in inducing those who are able to respond to this appeal. Let me therefore, in conclusion, recapitulate categorically what I believe is needed:

1 An industrial census, that we may know, for the whole city, the true facts.

2 Legislation that will abolish the rear tenement and the out-of-door-closet and will create breathing places for the people.
3 Philanthropically minded men and women who are willing, individually or collectively, to run the risk of possible meagre financial returns for the sake of leading the movement for model dwellings.
4 Closer study and examination of actual conditions by individuals, such as might be accomplished through a system of friendly rent collection.

Of your sympathy, I was certain at the outset; the lack of at least some knowledge of facts I trust no one of you may hereafter plead. May I hope that the paper of the afternoon may enable you to form clearer conceptions of your duty towards those 'Below the Hill.'

APPROXIMATE ANNUAL STATEMENT
FOR DIAMOND COURT PROPERTY

RECEIPTS	PER ANNUM
1 Store at $15.00 per month .	$ 180.00
1 Dwelling of 6 rooms at $3.00 per week	150.00
2 Dwelling of 6 rooms at 2.75 per week	275.00
4 Dwelling of 5 rooms at 2.50 per week	500.00
2 Dwelling of 4 rooms at 2.25 per week (special)	225.00
20 Dwelling of 4 rooms at 2.00 per week	2000.00
6 Dwelling of 3 rooms at 1.75 per week	525.00
2 Dwelling of 3 rooms at 1.60 per week	160.00
2 Dwelling of 3 rooms at 1.50 per week	150.00
Total possible revenue	$4165.00

EXPENDITURE

Interest on Mortgage 4½% on $16000	$ 720.00
Taxes	560.00
Water rates	220.00
Fire insurance	62.50
Light	100.00
Rent collecting	187.50
Janitor and supplies	125.00
Repairs and renewals	150.00
Sundries	50.00
5% on $36,500 capital investment	1825.00
Loss through vacancy and bad debts	165.00
	$4165.00